Taunton's

Container Garden

IDEA BOOK

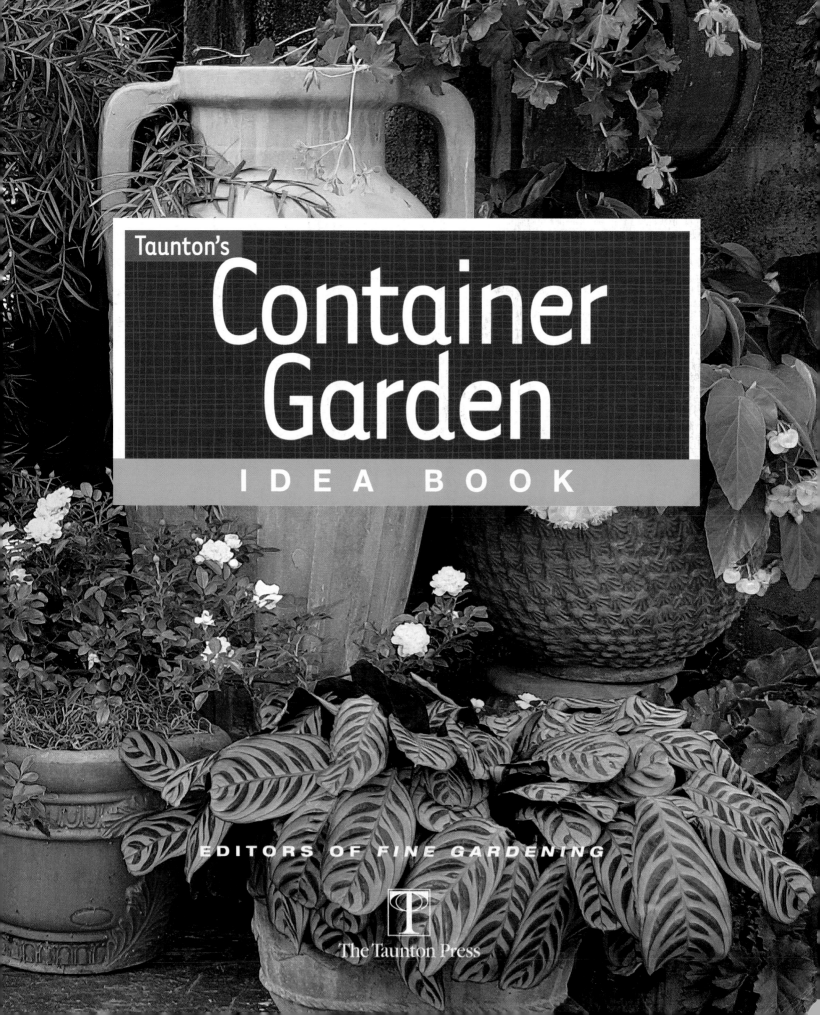

Taunton's

Container
Garden

IDEA BOOK

EDITORS OF FINE GARDENING

The Taunton Press

The Taunton Press
Inspiration for hands-on living®

The Taunton Press, Inc.
63 South Main Street, PO Box 5506
Newtown, CT 06470-5506
e-mail: tp@taunton.com

Editor: Lee Anne White
Copy editor: Valerie Cimino
Indexer: Jim Curtis
Cover design: Kimberly Adis
Interior design: Kimberly Adis
Layout: David Giammattei
Illustrator: Tinsley Morrison
Cover photographers: (Front cover, clockwise from top): Lee Anne White; Mick Hales; Mick Hales;
(Back cover, clockwise from top): courtesy of Margie Grace; Lee Anne White; Jennifer Benner, courtesy of
Fine Gardening, © The Taunton Press, Inc.; Steve Silk

Fine Gardening® is a trademark of The Taunton Press, Inc., registered in the U.S. Patent and Trademark Office.

The following names/manufacturers appearing in *Container Garden Idea Book* are trademarks: Angleface®
Wedgwood Blue summer snapdragon, Avalanche™ Rose petunia, Big Red Judy® coleus, Bonfire® begonia,
Callie® Orange calibrachoa, Caribbean Sunset™ cuphea, Catalins® Gilded Grape torenia, Compact Innocence®
nemesia, Dark Dancer™ white clover, Dazzler™ Mix impatiens, Dazzler™ Rose impatiens, Diamond Frost®
euphorbia, Dragon Wing® begonia, Dream Catcher™ kolkwitzia, Dream Kisses® Orange Sunset calibrachoa,
Festival Grass™, Ice Blue® podocarpus, King Tut® papyrus, Million Bells® calibrachoa, Million Bells® Terra Cotta
calibrachoa, Molten Lava™ oxalis, Napoleon™ papyrus, Nonstop® Yellow tuberous begonia, Painted Paradise™
Pink Improved New Guinea impatiens, Painted Paradise™ Red New Guinea impatiens, Panola™ Primrose
pansy, Petit Bleu™ blue-mist shrub, Razzle Dazzle® Cherry Dazzle® dwarf crape myrtle, Scopia™ Gulliver
White bacopa, Shadow Dancer® Violette fuchsia, Snowstorm® Giant Snowflake®, Soprano® Purple African
daisy, Sugar Tip® rose of Sharon, Superbells® Blue calibrachoa, Superbells® Coral calibrachoa, Superbells®
Red calibrachoa, Super Elfin™ Mix Pastel impatiens, Tiger Eyes® cutleaf staghorn sumac, Tiger Eyes™ sumac,
Tropicanna® canna, Walkabout Sunset® lysimachia, Wink™ Garnet diascia.

Library of Congress Cataloging-in-Publication Data
Container garden idea book / editors and contributors of Fine gardening.
    p. cm.
  Includes index.
  ISBN 978-1-60085-395-1
  1. Container gardening. 2. Plants, Potted. I. Fine gardening.
  SB418.C643 20011
  635.986--dc23
                    2011039815

Printed in the United States of America
10 9 8 7 6 5 4 3 2 1

contents

introduction

CONTAINER GARDENING IS THE MOST democratic form of gardening I know. It is accessible to everyone, whether they own a piece of land or not. It can be enjoyed by the young and old alike. And it can be equally engaging for those planting their first flowers or those with 50 years of serious gardening experience under their belt. Container gardening is a great option for those who are handicapped, who live in the city with only a balcony or sunny windowsill, or who have minimal time in which to maintain a garden. You can start with a few seeds and recycled containers if you're gardening on a budget or invest in a collection of elegant pots to host your plants and enhance any home.

It is the creative aspect of container gardening that I love the most. Container gardening is fun, and because what you plant isn't permanent, it provides the perfect opportunity to play in the garden. Mix and match plants. Move pots around to create new combinations. Try a plant in a pot before you place it more permanently in the ground.

Grow annuals, perennials, herbs, succulents, shrubs, trees, or whatever your heart desires. Showcase a new color scheme each year. Or move containers about as plants come in and out of their peak season to create an ever-changing display that always looks great. With container gardening, there are no mistakes, only experiments!

In this book, you'll learn about the basics of container gardening—everything from choosing containers to potting up plants and keeping them healthy. You'll also learn a range of strategies for design—whether you place one plant in a pot or pack your planters with a dozen perennials. You'll discover ways to use containers throughout the landscape—on the terrace, around the pool deck, on a rooftop, beckoning visitors to your front door, or as an architectural accent in a border. So pull on your gardening gloves, grab your spade, and start planning and planting!

—Lee Anne White

choosing the right containers

YOU CAN'T HAVE A CONTAINER GARDEN WITHOUT CONTAINERS. WHILE all containers must serve the utilitarian role of holding plants, soil, and water, they can also star in the garden—setting the tone, inspiring a color scheme, or establishing a sense of style. Their design is often just as important as the plants that grow in them. Choose from an amazing array of containers to enhance any home, to suit any gardening style, and to hold just about any plant.

Inexpensive pots can function equally as well as their pricier cousins, so consider spending your container budget where it matters most, choosing decorative containers for key locations like entryways or where the pots will be seen even after the plants have filled in. Opt for inexpensive containers when they will be camouflaged by trailing plants or otherwise screened from view.

Also, don't forget to adapt and recycle. After all, just about anything that can hold soil and plants and provide for drainage can serve as a container. Look around your home or the hardware store. Baskets can be lined with plastic and coco fiber so they will hold soil and moisture. Holes can be drilled for drainage in boxes or hollowed-out logs. And don't forget that containers can be hung from eaves or mounted beneath windows as well as placed on a terrace or in the garden.

Containers can be easily mixed and matched. Here, a cluster of three ceramic and terra-cotta pots filled with spider flower and petunias call attention to a grade change in a sunny backyard.

basic considerations

●●● THERE IS MORE TO CONTAINERS THAN GOOD LOOKS. First and foremost, containers must be able to hold ample soil and water while allowing excess moisture to drain out. They must be large enough to give roots plenty of room to grow, yet ideally light enough to move when filled with soil and plants. And they must be durable as well—capable of lasting through the years and withstanding local freeze-thaw cycles if left outdoors over winter.

Plant roots can quickly fill a pot, so look for a pot that is bigger than you think you might need. Also, make sure that your container has drainage holes so that excess water, particularly after a good soaking, can run out the bottom. A bit of screen or mesh over the hole will keep the soil from washing away at the same time.

Baskets don't last very long when left out in the weather, but they certainly make charming containers. They can be lined with plastic to give them a longer lifespan.

These large, heavy tubs aren't going anywhere. They deserve a permanent place in the garden because they would be difficult to move even with a hand truck. A trailing ornamental oregano sports billowing pink blossoms.

1. Golden Italian cypress (*Cupressus sempervirens* 'Swane's Gold', Zones 7-9)

2. 'Mystic Illusion' dahlia (*Dahlia* 'Mystic Illusion', Zones 9-11)

3. Festival Grass™ cordyline (*Cordyline* 'Jurred', Zones 9-11)

4. Purple heart (*Tradescantia pallida* 'Purpurea', Zones 8-11)

5. Dinosaur kale (*Irassica oleracea* 'Nero di Toscana', annual)

•capacity and drainage

Most plants have deep roots, so if you'll be placing a single plant in a pot, select a container that is deeper than it is wide. For multiple plants, choose pots both deep and wide. And for those plants with minimal root systems, such as succulents and spreading, groundcover-type plants, choose shallow containers—a deep pot would simply waste potting soil. Even so, larger pots are almost always better than small pots. They reduce the need to repot plants frequently by giving roots plenty of room in which to grow. Equally important is their capacity to hold moisture. The smaller the pot, the more often it has to be watered.

TOP This pot may not have drainage holes in the bottom, but there is plenty of room for excess water to seep out through its sides. Lining the pot with dark mesh or moss helps keep soil from spilling out.

RIGHT Wire baskets can be lined with sphagnum moss, then filled with soil and plants. Here, sweet alyssum, grape hyacinths, and purple osteospermum combine to create a charming spring arrangement that can be easily moved about the garden.

adding a drainage hole

most pots have drainage holes, but if yours doesn't, use a masonry bit to drill a ½-inch-diameter hole in the center of the bottom of the vessel. Don't rush the job. It can take time to drill through a thick ceramic pot, and you don't want to risk cracking the container. Consider adding a small piece of screen over the hole to allow water out while keeping the potting soil contained.

Large pots hold lots of plants, ample soil, and plenty of water. This one is also situated in shade. The combination of large pot and shady site means this pot won't have to be watered very often.

•durability

All containers are not created equal, at least not when it comes to durability. For a pot that's going to last, know the pros and cons of its construction. Terra-cotta, while great in warm climates, must be protected in areas with harsh winters to prevent cracking and flaking. And all clay or ceramic pots, despite their beauty, will break when dropped. Wooden containers will last for years, but must be carefully maintained to prevent premature rotting. Concrete containers are almost indestructible, yet they will still chip when bumped or dropped. Stone planters, while expensive, are durable and attractive. Many of the newer, synthetic pots that look like they are made from cement, stone, or clay offer durable, lightweight, and affordable alternatives.

The glaze on this ceramic pot adds to its durability. However, the narrow neck reduces its ability to withstand cold winters. If damp soil inside the pot expands when frozen, it can't slip upward as it might in a graduated, smooth-sided container.

High-fired terra-cotta containers from Europe are both decorative and durable. Their thick, dense walls absorb less moisture than common terra-cotta, which means they are less likely to suffer from winter freeze damage.

pot feet help prevent freeze damage

freezing temperatures make it absolutely necessary to lift containers off the ground to keep the base from freezing and breaking. Pot feet do the lifting and ensure that potentially freezing water will drain off quickly and not collect in or under the container.

—Rita Randolph

• size and weight

Although larger pots generally provide better growing conditions than smaller pots, their weight can be an issue when filled with plants, soil, and water— especially if placed on a deck, balcony, or rooftop. Under these conditions, seek out lightweight alternatives such as synthetic pots. However, if you're growing trees or other large plants that might topple in a storm, go for large, heavy pots made of concrete and stone and plan to leave them in place, if possible. Moving such pots even short distances can be a challenge. Lifting them up and down steps can require several able-bodied helpers. If you frequently rearrange your containers, a good hand truck may be your best investment of all.

TOP Although tall and heavy, these pots make a visual statement anchoring the corner of a patio. They can be easily moved with a hand truck.

RIGHT Medium-sized plants grow well in medium-sized pots. These succulents have small root systems.

sizeable pots give plants room to grow

1. Tiger Eyes™ sumac
   (*Rhus typhina* 'Bailtiger',
   Zones 4-8)

2. 'Double Purple' devil's
   trumpet (*Datura metel*
   'Double Purple',
   Zones 9-11)

3. Catalins® Gilded Grape
   torenia (*Torenia* 'Dancat
   266', annual)

4. Blue echeveria (*Echeveria
   secunda* var. *glauca,*
   Zones 9-11)

5. 'Kent Beauty' ornamental
   oregano (*Origanum* 'Kent
   Beauty', Zones 5-8)

containers
with style

●●● THERE'S A CONTAINER FOR ANY STYLE GARDEN, whether classic, contemporary, or eclectic. When selecting a container style, start by taking cues from the surroundings. Natural wood planters might enhance a cedar home, while metal containers might complement more contemporary architecture. Terracotta, ceramic, concrete, and stone containers suit more traditional garden settings. Often, style has as much to do with the decoration on the container as the material it is made from. And you can choose from clean, simple lines or more intriguing shapes, such as tall tapers, urns, or long box planters. Found objects—from corrugated pipes to wire baskets to old pails—can always be put to good use in the right setting.

ABOVE This fern-filled container doubles as garden statuary. Its style signals a formal garden setting, while the choice of plant signals shade. Placing the container atop a concrete pedestal adds to the formal ambience.

RIGHT This classic planter box is large enough to support a small crabapple and is ideally suited to a traditional or English-style landscape.

unique pot glazing inspires a color combination

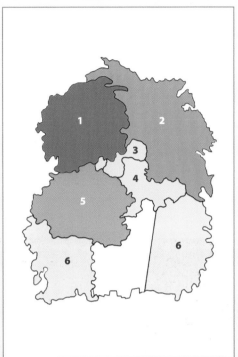

1. 'Peter's Wonder' coleus (*Solenostemon scutellarioides* 'Peter's Wonder', Zone 11)

2. 'Stained Glass' coleus (*Solenostemon scutellarioides* 'Stained Glass', Zone 11)

3. 'Persian Queen' geranium (*Pelargonium* 'Persian Queen', annual)

4. Walkabout Sunset® lysimachia (*Lysimachia congestiflora* Walkabout Sunset®, Zones 7-11)

5. Superbells® Coral calibrachoa (*Calibrachoa* Superbells®, annual)

6. Snowstorm® Giant Snowflake® bacopa (*Sutera cordata* Snowstorm® Giant Snowflake®, annual)

• classic containers

Container plantings have long been elements of classic gardens. It's not just the style of the container itself that makes it classic but also the way it is planted and placed in the landscape. Classic containers run the gamut from rolled-rim terra-cotta pots and painted box planters to more formal iron urns and cast-stone jardinières. When using a container as a focal point, choose large pots whose scale makes a statement in the landscape. Place two planters symmetrically balanced on either side of an entry. Or line an allée or walkway with a row of matching planters. Classic shapes and decorative surfaces also contribute to the impression these containers make in the garden.

ABOVE Both the paneled design and white paint signal that this window box is a classic. It is planted formally with swags of trailing ivy, ferns, and other foliage plants that thrive in shade.

BELOW The placement of this pot and the clipped boxwood planted in it signal that this is a formal garden. The pot blends right in with the dwarf boxwood parterre in the courtyard garden.

metal urn conjures up an old-fashioned feeling

1. Full-moon maple (*Acer japonicum* 'Aconitifolium', Zones 5-7)

2. African mask (*Alocasia* x *amazonica*, Zones 10-11)

3. 'Limelight' licorice plant (*Helichrysum petiolare* 'Limelight', Zones 10-11)

4. 'Troy's Gold' plectranthus (*Plectranthus ciliatus* 'Troy's Gold', Zones 10-11)

5. Diamond Frost® euphorbia (*Euphorbia* 'Inneuphdia', Zones 10-11)

6. Tazmanian tree fern (*Dicksonia antarctica*, Zones 9-11)

7. Dream Catcher™ kolkwitzia (*Kolkwitzia amabilis* Dream Catcher™, Zones 5-8)

8. 'Wojo's Jem' vinca (*Vinca maculata* 'Wojo's Jem', Zones 7-10)

• contemporary pots

Clean lines are the hallmark of contemporary gardens. Often sleek and shiny or finished in bold colors, contemporary pots make a strong statement in landscapes that tend to be sparsely yet boldly planted. Indeed, the pots themselves play an important role and are often highlighted rather than covered with trailing plants. Unfinished construction materials such as rusted iron sheets and corrugated metal can also be fashioned into contemporary pots and planters. Such planters are often paired with either bold or understated plants—from striking drumstick alliums and dramatic succulents to soft, flowing ornamental grasses and simple groundcovers. While flowers are always welcome, foliage frequently plays a starring role in contemporary gardens.

ABOVE These matching ceramic pots have updated lines that blend in well with more modern architecture and a gray finish that complements most other colors. They greet guests on this landing by the front door.

TOP LEFT Contemporary corrugated metal pots are quite adaptable, blending in with varied garden styles. This one is bucket sized, filled with Calliente® Orange geranium and Techno® Heat light blue lobelia and placed in a shady woodland garden to provide a spot of color.

an iron bowl anchors a contemporary deck

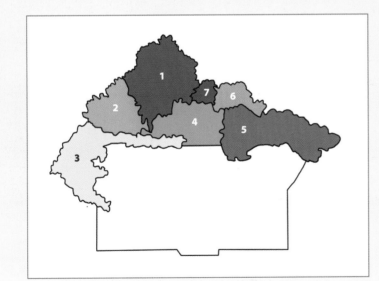

1. Miniature pine tree (*Crassula tetragona*, Zones 10-11)

2. Coppertone sedum (*Sedum nussbaumerianum*, Zones 10-11)

3. Crassula (*Crassula pellucida*, Zones 10-11)

4. 'Silver Spoons' echeveria (*Echeveria* 'Silver Spoons, Zones 9-11)

5. Trailing jade (*Senecia jacobsenii*, Zones 9-11)

6. Flower dust plant (*Kalanchoe pumila*, Zones 10-11)

7. 'Hobbit' dwarf jade (*Crassula ovata* 'Hobbit', Zone 11)

• planters, tubs, and barrels

Box planters, tubs, and barrels come in a range of styles from classic to contemporary, but most often tend to be more rustic in character. Half whiskey barrels or their lighter-weight cousins, garden tubs, can be found in garden centers and are ideal for shrubs, trees, sprawling plants, or multiple plants, as well as vegetables that need room to ramble. Planter boxes are great for edging a terrace, anchoring a porch, or defining the walls between garden rooms. Large metal tubs, troughs, and feeders from the farm store can also be converted into generously sized containers and are perfect for container water gardens.

watering containers

Watering is the trickiest chore because it is weather dependent. The hotter the temperature, the more often you have to water. The rate of evaporation depends on the pot. A big container retains moisture longer than a small one. Also, plastic pots hold moisture longer than porous clay and wooden containers.

I water my pots almost every day from June to September. As the weather gets cooler and the days get shorter, I water less often. Always soak the soil thoroughly; water should run out of the drainage holes. Allow the plants to use up that water before you add more, and always empty out any excess water if you use saucers under your pots, as standing water is a death sentence to most potted plants.

—Sydney Eddison

FACING PAGE Troughs need not have served a previous life on a farm. Old decorative objects found in flea markets, antique stores, or your attic can do double duty as trough-sized planters. This one anchors a collection of pots on a shady patio and is filled with an assortment of ferns.

TOP This rectangular box planter is classic in style, built from wood, and painted to blend with the architecture and landscape. It is placed along the edge of a low stone deck, where it doubles as a safety barrier.

LEFT Old whiskey barrels have always been favorites for growing vegetables, but they work for ornamentals like these clipped rosemary bushes as well. The wood blends in with the surrounding rhododendron arbors and fences.

•eclectic containers

The search for eclectic containers can spark the imagination. Look through your garage, attic, basement, and storage closets to see what you can find. Baskets, boxes, buckets, old watering cans, and more can be converted to planters. Hardware stores, flea markets, and antique stores are also great places for affordable finds. If the containers don't offer drainage, drill or punch a few holes in the bottom. If they are made from wire, fill them first with coco fiber to hold soil and help retain water. Eclectic container gardens are often filled with texture and color, with multiple plants in a pot or groups of pots clustered together. They are playful, original, and make great conversation starters.

This chair was wrapped in sphagnum moss, with a basin of soil provided in the seat. Plants and vines can scramble over the chair, eventually covering it with greenery.

An unusual container was constructed from sheet metal that was cut, bent, and soldered together before being painted. It adds a note of whimsy and an upright accent to this colorful garden.

ABOVE This bait bucket is enjoying a second life as a garden container. It's perfect for succulents because the holes provide excellent drainage.

LEFT The owner of this garden made her own face jug container in a pottery class. Filled with succulents, it offers an element of surprise when discovered tucked into a border.

window boxes and hanging baskets

Window boxes and hanging baskets are both long-time favorites with gardeners and homeowners alike. They each require special considerations because they are hung rather than placed on the ground. Their size is limited by weight and what walls, beams, railings, or eaves can realistically handle. Despite their smaller size, window boxes and hanging baskets are often packed with as many plants as possible, then allowed to sprawl, spill, and cascade toward the ground. This combination of smaller container and dense planting means that daily water is essential, and planters in full sun may need more than one soaking a day, so easy access to water or a drip-irrigation system is a must for plants to thrive.

Hanging baskets come in a variety of shapes and sizes. This one was designed to hang against a wall or from a deck railing. The dark pink impatiens and golden creeping Jenny draw your eye not only to the container but also to the lake view beyond.

This shady window box spruces up the front porch of a pool house where swimmers seek refuge from the summer sun. It's packed with 10 plants—a combination of upright, mounding, and trailing selections.

Window boxes don't have to hang beneath windows. They can also be hung on deck railing or fencing, as they are here. Grouping multiple window boxes together makes a bold street-side impression.

fetching pansies for spring and fall

LATIN NAME	FLOWER SIZE	COLOR	BLOOM TIME
Viola x *wittrockiana* 'Atlas Black'	Large	Black	Early spring
V. x *wittrockiana* Character series	Large	Solid, multicolor	Spring to fall
V. x *wittrockiana* Delta series	Medium to large	Pastels, bright-colored	Early spring
V. x *wittrockiana* Icicle series	Medium	Vibrant	Fall, early spring
V. x *wittrockiana* Imperial series	Large	Unusual, warm pastels	Early spring to midsummer
V. x *wittrockiana* 'Joker Poker Face'	Medium	Orange, purple	Early spring
V. x *wittrockiana* 'Jolly Joker'	Medium	Orange-purple multicolor	Late spring, summer
V. x *wittrockiana* Majestic Giants series	Large	Pastel to vibrant	Early spring
V. x *wittrockiana* 'Padparadja'	Medium	Deep, bright orange	Early spring to fall
V. x *wittrockiana* Panola Panache series	Miniature	Wide color & marking range	Spring, fall
V. x *wittrockiana* Victorian series	Medium	Multicolor	Early spring

—*Cynthia M. Rabinowitz*

Majestic Giant series

Imperial series

'Padparadja'

materials

●●● THE RANGE OF MATERIALS USED TO make pots and planters has changed dramatically in recent years. While iron, terra-cotta, and wooden planters have remained popular for centuries, many new, synthetic materials such as foam, resin, and molded plastic are equally elegant, featherweight by comparison, and surprisingly durable. Contemporary architecture has also spurred the production of garden containers made from steel and other metals. These various materials come in a variety of textures and colors, resulting in a wide range of choices when it comes to selecting the containers for the landscape. The range in colors of glazed ceramic pots alone is enough to excite and challenge any gardener, so keep in mind that most gardens benefit from a limited color scheme. While some enjoy playing with bold color schemes, others prefer natural, earthy colors that allow the plants to shine.

ABOVE Hypertufa troughs are made from a mix of sand, peat moss, and Portland cement. They are available commercially in a range of shapes and sizes, or you can make your own using cardboard boxes as forms.

RIGHT This large bowl was fabricated from iron. The rusting patina blends nicely with brick and other earthy tones found in the garden. If desired, iron bowls and basins can be powder-coated for a more polished finish.

aquamarine glaze anchors an aquatic setting

1. 'Gracillimus' miscanthus (*Miscanthus sinensis* 'Gracillimus', Zones 4-9)

2. 'Sweet Caroline Purple' sweet potato vine (*Ipomea batatas* 'Sweet Caroline Purple', Zone 11)

3. Variegated potato vine (*Solanum jasminoides* 'Variegata', Zones 9-11)

4. Dwarf yellow dahlia (*Dahlia* cv., Zones 9-11)

5. 'Pesto Perpetuo' variegated basil (*Ocimum* x *citriodorum* 'Pesto Perpetuo', annual)

6. Trailing rosemary (*Rosmarinus officinalis* 'Prostratus', Zones 8-11)

7. Spicy globe basil (*Ocimum basilicum* 'Spicy Globe', annual)

8. Sweet bay (*Laurus nobilis*, Zones 8-11)

9. 'Silver Falls' dichondra (*Dichondra argentea* 'Silver Falls', Zones 10-11)

10. 'Firecracker' fuchsia (*Fuchsia triphylla* 'Firecracker', Zones 10-11)

11. Purple heart (*Tradescantia pallida* 'Purpurea', Zones 8-11)

12. 'Sunset Velvet' oxalis (*Oxalis siliquosa* 'Sunset Velvet', Zones 8-10)

• terra-cotta

Terra-cotta is the most traditional and common type of garden container. It is both attractive and affordable and comes in a wide range of shapes and sizes. Most of these containers are simple in design, but others have rolled edges or other decorative elements. One of terra-cotta's benefits is its porosity, which allows plant roots to breathe. For this same reason, it can be fairly quick to dry out in summer heat or high winds. High-fired terra-cotta, which usually comes from Europe, has a smooth surface and is more durable. Low-fired terra-cotta from Mexico tends to have a rough surface that gives it an appealing rustic appearance, yet it lacks the durability required in cold climates.

Impruneta terra-cotta from Italy's Tuscany region is considered the finest terra-cotta in the world. Its thick walls and dense firing make it the most durable as well.

overwintering pots

because we have long, cold winters where I live in Connecticut, I move some tender plants indoors for the winter and take cuttings of others, like my beloved *Brugmansia.* Eventually Jack Frost gets the rest. Plant remains go to the compost pile, and I use the spent soil to fill holes in the lawn. I store some of my pots in a shed. Since space is at a premium, I keep the others in one of those ready-made, shedlike enclosures for garbage cans. The addition of a shelf inside increases the storage space. Large wood and plastic planters, which can stand the rigors of winter, do not need to be stored in a covered space.

—Sydney Eddison

Broken pots have their place in the garden, too. Partially buried and filled with soil and plants, they add a sculptural element to beds and borders.

Big buildings deserve big pots, like this oversized, rolled-rim terra-cotta pot filled with pink petunias that marks the entry to a big red barn. A pot this size doesn't get moved around much.

• wood

Wood containers are a natural choice for the
landscape. They can be built into benches or
enhanced with trellises to add an upright accent
to the garden. Cedar, redwood, and teak are most
commonly used to construct wooden containers,
as they are rot resistant and weather to a beautiful
patina. Other lumbers can also be used and painted
to complement a color scheme. When shopping, look
for sturdy wooden planters with well-constructed,
solid joints. Even rot-resistant woods will eventually
decay, so extend the life of a wooden planter by
lining it with plastic, ensuring that it has adequate
drainage, and treating it with a nontoxic stain, paint,
or waterproof sealer. If necessary, reinforce the joints
with galvanized screws.

**In a rustic setting, such as a cabin or potting shed, a simply
constructed wooden box made from scrap lumber offers
charm and an affordable alternative to more expensive rot-
resistant woods.**

**Wooden boxes
can be painted to
match surrounding
architectural
elements such as
doors, shutters, or
trim. The paint has
the added benefit
of extending the
life of the container,
although it must be
repainted periodically.**

A portable potting operation

Clay, wood, and ceramic pots filled with soil and plants can be heavy to move, so I've developed a portable potting operation that allows me to plant pots at their intended destination rather than at a remote potting bench. The key to my operation is a large wheelbarrow dedicated solely to the purpose. I fill it with potting soil, mixing in other amendments (such as compost and slow-release fertilizer), and then I roll the wheelbarrow around from pot to pot. I can also roll it to the nearest hose to moisten the soil.

I keep a small shovel, trowel, and pair of gloves in the wheelbarrow for convenience. I can even place plants on top to transport them from the car to their final destination. At the end of the day, I simply roll the wheelbarrow back into the shed and cover the soil with a drop cloth to help keep the soil moist.

—Lee Anne White

Teak planter boxes come in a range of styles and sizes, from classic to contemporary. A fresh coat of sealer each spring keeps them looking fresh. Left unsealed, they will weather to a nice patina.

•glazed ceramic

Glazed ceramic pots generally hail from Asia and the South Pacific. They feature colorful exterior glazes to match any color scheme. Although they require extra care and must be brought in for the winter in harsh climates, many of these stoneware pots have thick walls and heavy glazes, making them considerably more durable than terra-cotta pots. Still, they will chip and break, so are better suited to moderate climates than areas that experience frequent winter rains followed by freezing temperatures. Brightly colored pots can liven up any garden setting, while earthy-looking glazes can help create a rustic or naturalistic atmosphere. Such pots are also ideal in Japanese-style gardens.

ABOVE These large, thick-walled ceramic pots stand nearly 4 feet tall along the edge of a limestone patio. Both the containers and the matching yucca plants create an element of repetition in the landscape.

LEFT These glazed ceramic containers can sit outside year-round in moderate climates or under shelter where the gardener can postpone watering if a hard freeze is expected. Glazed terra-cotta containers are often sold as sets of different-sized pots, which makes for an interesting arrangement.

ceramic pot provides colorful, textural accent

1. Taro (*Colocasia esculenta* 'Illustris', Zones 8-11)

2. New Guinea impatiens (*Impatiens* 'Riviera Pastel Pink', annual)

3. Fuchsia (*Fuchsia* 'Autumnale', Zones 9-11)

• metal

Iron urns have been around for ages, but newer metal containers offer an interesting alternative to traditional pots, especially in contemporary settings. Choose from aluminum, galvanized steel, stainless steel, or copper construction, as well as smooth, hammered, brushed, or colored finishes in an assortment of shapes and sizes. Copper containers can be sealed to protect their rich, metallic finish or allowed to weather to a blue-green patina, and they should be lined to prevent copper oxide from leaching into potting soil. Empty paint cans or old pails and buckets can also be placed into service as containers. Keep in mind that metal can heat up in sunny locations, so they are best used in shadier sites or cooler climates where plant roots won't become scorched.

TOP This iron urn was painted bright blue to contrast with the sunny yellow foliage of a Walkabout Sunset® lysimachia. Both the color and plant choice offer an unexpected update to a classic container.

RIGHT These iron planters were fabricated to fit a narrow side-yard passageway, bringing plantings up closer to eye level. This also exposed the plants to more a bit more sunlight. It was an ingenious solution to a challenging spot in the landscape.

EYE-CATCHING COMBINATIONS

1. Variegated agave (*Agave americana* 'Marginata', Zones 9-11)

2. Diamond Frost® euphorbia (*Euphorbia* 'Inneuphdia', Zones 10-11)

3. 'Ogon' sedum (*Sedum makinoi* 'Ogon', Zones 6-9)

cast-stone planter serves as a focal point

1. Variegated flax lily (*Dianella tasmanica* 'Variegata', Zones 9-11)

2. Pinks (*Dianthus deltoides*, Zones 3-9)

uSDA Hardiness Zones refer to a plant's expected winter hardiness when planted in the ground. Exposed in containers, a plant may even lose a zone of hardiness because it has less insulation. While that may make you think twice about planting a nonhardy plant in the ground, it shouldn't stop you from playing with them in containers. They will still grow; they just won't survive cold winters outside of their zone. Simply treat them as annuals. Enjoy them all summer and toss them at the end of the season, or experiment with ways to overwinter them indoors if you don't have a greenhouse.

• concrete and cast stone

Concrete and cast stone are the heaviest and most durable of containers. They are excellent in windy locations or with top-heavy plants such as trees or bamboo that would topple lighter alternatives. And they can be left outdoors in even the harshest winters, which is a benefit since even moderate-sized concrete and cast-stone containers can be a challenge to move. Although they can chip, it's nearly impossible to break them. They may be smooth-sided with rounded rims or designed with a decorative, three-dimensional surface, and they acquire a rich patina over time when exposed to moisture and moss. Hypertufa is a related material made from sand, peat moss, and Portland cement that can be used to create an inexpensive, rustic container.

ABOVE This alpine trough was handmade from hypertufa—an easy weekend project. It is filled with dwarf rock garden plants like sedum, dwarf mondo grass, a boxleaf honeysuckle, 'Butterscotch' euonymus, and a 'Fernspray' hinoki cypress.

TOP LEFT Concrete planters can be stained with pigments and cast in forms to create decorative motifs such as this dragonfly. Red geraniums add a colorful accent to this otherwise earth-tone setting.

•synthetic materials

Synthetic pots are lightweight, durable, waterproof, rot-proof, impact-resistant, and often frost-resistant, making them ideal for rooftop gardens, balconies, and anywhere weight is a concern. They also require little or no care. Because of their ease of manufacture, many synthetic pots are less expensive than or at least comparable in price to other types of containers. They are available in a comprehensive range of shapes, sizes, and colors, and can be made from heavy molded plastic, glass-reinforced plastic (GRP), advanced composites (AC), fiberglass, resin, and polyurethane foam; all of these materials can be molded into classic and contemporary shapes. In fact, sometimes it's hard to tell the difference between a synthetic pot and more natural materials such as terra-cotta and wood. An added benefit is that many synthetic containers include self-watering reservoirs that reduce the frequency of watering.

TOP This gardenia is a classic plant for a classic-looking pot. Made from foam, this lightweight pot provides a thick layer of insulation, protecting plant roots from extreme temperature swings.

RIGHT Colorful pots add a perfect accent around a pool. This one made from molded plastic was the largest in a nested, three-pot set. Pots like this are readily available in a range of colors at your local home center.

FAR RIGHT A 'Red Wing' viburnum makes its home in this large resin pot. The resin can withstand cold winters, and the generous capacity of the container means that this shrub won't have to be repotted or transplanted to the garden for several years.

plant forms echo the curves of a plastic pot

1. 'Giant Glutinosum' aeonium (*Aeonium* 'Giant Glutinosum', Zones 9-11)

2. Sedum (*Sedum* cv., Zones 6-11)

3. Echeveria (*Echeveria* sp., Zone 11)

designing container plantings

• • •

IT'S HARD TO GO WRONG WHEN GARDENING IN CONTAINERS. It's the perfect place for a first garden, because it's so easy to experiment with different plant combinations. And it's that same opportunity for playfulness that appeals to even the most sophisticated designers. Start simply or dare to be dramatic. If something doesn't work, just shift things around or start fresh next year.

It is this ability to move pots about that makes container design so interesting. In essence, there are three key aspects of container garden design: how plants are arranged within a container, how multiple containers relate to each other, and how container plantings relate to the surrounding landscape and architecture. Place pots as focal points in the garden or landscape, group them in clusters, or arrange them to create screens or walls.

A key decision is whether to place one plant in a pot cluster for a pleasing composition or to place multiple plants in a single pot to create a dramatic focal point. Both strategies work equally well, as does mixing and matching the two. Experimenting with containers is a great way to discover new plant combinations for use in the garden. In fact, as plants outgrow their pots, they often benefit from a more permanent home in the landscape.

With the right combination of foliage and flowers, a single container can be just as lush as plantings in a border. The bold Tropicanna® canna and 'Black Magic' elephant's ear call attention to the pot, while the color of the Callie® Orange calibrachoa, sweet potato vine, and black-eyed Susan keep the eye engaged.

design basics

●●● GARDEN DESIGN IS AN ART FORM. It draws upon the basic design elements of space, line, color, shape, form, and texture, which apply not only to the plants' leaves, flowers, and overall form but also to the containers and groupings of containers. The same design principles used in other forms of art apply as well. Combine various shapes, textures, colors, and forms to create balance, rhythm, contrast, proportion, and unity. Container gardening is an exciting way to learn about design and to experiment with these principles on a small scale in the landscape.

What makes garden design—whether in a pot or in the ground—different is the element of time. In addition to looking at how plants work together when they are planted, you must imagine how they will look together once they've had time to grow and how they will change through the seasons. But this is what makes gardening such a pleasure. Each day brings a new discovery and delight in the landscape.

ABOVE Anchored by the green-and-white-striped leaves of 'Winning Streak' ornamental corn that dance about the container, this densely packed planting showcases a mix of solid green, colored, and variegated foliage and is punctuated by purple and orange flowers.

RIGHT The repetition of crisp, white daffodils and stalks of purple hyacinth create a bold, eye-catching container display in early spring. Although simple in design and color scheme, the container plantings provide a dramatic contrast to the surrounding clipped evergreen parterres.

orange is hot, hot, hot!

1. Tiger Eyes® cutleaf staghorn sumac (*Rhus typhina* 'Bailtiger', Zones 4-8)

2. 'Sedona' coleus (*Solenostemon scutellarioides* 'Sedona', Zone 11)

3. Big Red Judy® coleus (*Solenstemon scutellarioides* Big Red Judy®, Zone 11)

4. 'Black Scallop' bugleweed (*Ajuga reptans* 'Black Scallop', Zones 3-9)

5. Bonfire® begonia (*Begonia boliviensis* 'Nzcone', Zones 10-11)

pair a pot with its setting

1. 'Royal Purple' smoke bush (*Cotinus coggygria* 'Royal Purple', Zones 5-9)

2. Festival Grass™ cordyline (*Cordyline* Festival Grass™, Zones 9-11)

3. 'Southern Comfort' heuchera (*Heuchera* 'Southern Comfort', Zones 4-8)

4. 'Henna' coleus (*Solenostemon scutellarioides* 'Henna', Zones 11)

5. 'Profusion Fire' zinnia (*Zinnia* 'Profusion Fire', annual)

6. 'Blackie' sweet potato vine (*Ipomoea batatas* 'Blackie', Zone 11)

colorful foliage and flowers are a powerful mix

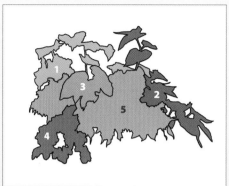

1. 'Thai Beauty' caladium (*Caladium bicolor* 'Thai Beauty', Zones 10-11)

2. 'Sinbad' cane begonia (*Begonia* 'Sinbad', Zone 11)

3. Angel wing begonia (*Begonia coccinea,* Zone 11)

4. 'Silver Scrolls' heuchera (*Heuchera* 'Silver Scrolls', Zones 4-9)

5. Super Elfin™ Mix Pastel impatiens (*Impatiens walleriana* Super Elfin™ Mix Pastel, annual)

ABOVE Petunias are an excellent choice for colorful, long-season containers. They have a rambling and trailing habit that contrasts nicely with upright foliage plants, and they often bloom for months at a time—though their spent flowers do need to be cleaned up.

LEFT Color is key in this composition, as the container's color is echoed in the plant foliage and fish sculpture. But the element of line, which provides a strong visual connection between the sculpture and the container planting, is what makes it truly compelling.

•shape and form

Shape, form, and *habit* are terms that are often tossed around interchangeably. In garden design, *shape* most often refers to the two-dimensional aspect, or "outline," of a plant, leaf, or flower, while *form* generally refers to its three-dimensional qualities. For instance, a leaf's shape might be circular, oval, palmate, or pinnate, while a shrub's form might be round, square, or naturalistic (irregular). *Habit* has more to do with the way a plant grows, or its *gesture*— sprawling, mounding, upright, columnar, loose, matting, trailing, or spiky. These individual features of plants—especially their leaves—can be contrasted or used repetitively to create an eye-catching container combination. A mix of habits, especially in a container with multiple plants, is also a key to design success.

Dramatically contrasting leaf shapes create an intriguing combination. The varying leaf color aids the composition as well. Pale 'Moonshine' mother-in-law's tongue shines as a companion for the darker-leaved coral bells.

The varied leaf forms add noticeable texture to this container combo. Compare the broad leaves of 'Blackie' sweet potato vine and 'Marine' heliotrope to the crinkled, leaves of 'Sofie Cascade' ivy geranium and the narrow, delicate foliage of Goldilocks Rocks'™ bideus feruifolia and Stratosphere™ White gaura.

a big-leaf, little-leaf combo

1. 'Siam Ruby' banana (*Musa acuminata* 'Siam Ruby', Zones 9-11)

2. 'Thailand Giant Strain' elephant's ears (*Colocasia gigantea* 'Thailand Giant Strain', Zones 8-11)

3. 'Panama Red' hibiscus (*Hibiscus acetosella* 'Panama Red', Zones 10-11)

4. 'Red Hot Rio' coleus (*Solenostemon scuttelarioides* 'Red Hot Rio', Zone 11)

pinch a plant

many plants benefit from a good pinching in spring. They become stronger, bushier plants as a result, for wherever you pinch back one stem, two stems will emerge from the node left behind. You might even be able to root the stems you pinched off, which means more plants for you. If you're doubtful, try this simple experiment: Buy two identical coleus (*Solenostemon scutellarioides* cvs.) plants in spring. Pinch one plant, but leave the other alone. Compare the two plants in August and decide for yourself.

The narrow, waxy leaves of purple heart contrast sharply with the fuzzy, serrated leaves of plectranthus and the almost beadlike foliage of a sedum. It is a combination that thrives in partial shade.

Although accented with a few red flowers, this combination of container plantings is clearly about the foliage. The scalloped, heart-shaped leaves of 'Rosalie' caladium offer a dramatic contrast to the nautilus-shaped, variegated leaves of 'Exotica' begonia. The surrounding green foliage expands the range of foliage shapes and sizes.

narrow leaves vary in habit

1. 'Dark Delight' New Zealand flax (*Phormium* 'Dark Delight', Zones 8-11)

2. Bamboo (*Phyllostachys* cv., Zones 5-11)

3. Blue oat grass (*Helictotrichon sempervirens*, Zones 4-9)

simple yet dramatic contrast sings

1. **Agave** (*Agave americana* 'Marginata', Zones 9-11)

2. **Woolly thyme** (*Thymus pseudolanuginosus*, Zones 5-9)

explore variations in leaf shape

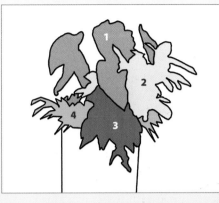

1. 'Illustris' elephant's ear (*Colocasia esculenta* 'Illustris', Zones 8-11)

2. Persian shield (*Strobilanthes dyerianus*, Zones 9-11)

3. Rex begonia vine (*Cissus discolor*, Zone 11)

4. Golden dwarf sweet flag (*Acorus gramineus* 'Ogon', Zones 6-9)

The leaves of these shade-loving plants vary in both shape and habit. The planting includes narrow-leaved sweet flag, sprawling spotted dead nettle, bold-leaved leopard plant, and an ovate-leaved coleus.

• texture

Great foliage is what gives containers long-season good looks, even after the flowers are gone. Many designers base container combinations strictly on foliage because of the drama it can create. One of the secrets to working with foliage is textural contrast, which can be either tactile or visual. *Tactile texture* is that which you can feel—fuzzy leaves, prickly spines, jagged leaf edges, and smooth leaf surfaces. *Visual texture* is more of an illusion that has to do with the introduction of many tiny or narrow leaves, especially when set against broader leaves. The greater the variety and the more extreme the contrast in either tactile or visual texture, the more dramatic the planting.

ABOVE Succulent plants vary widely in texture, as demonstrated by the smooth leaves of 'Lucy' echeveria and the needle-like foliage of 'Angelina' sedum. A smaller, gray-leaved 'Bertram Anderson' sedum fills the background.

RIGHT This planting combination offers both physical and visual texture. The leaves of bed of nails, also known as Naranjilla (*Solanum quitoense*), are thorny to touch.

Although there are a few flowers in bloom, it's clearly dramatic foliage textures that draw your eye to this cozy seating area. For example, there is stark contrast in texture between the upright horsetails and the bushy asparagus fern. This is the kind of garden that you want to reach out and touch.

fine and narrow leaves add visual texture

1. Tiger Eyes™ sumac (*Rhus typhina* 'Bailtiger', Zones 4-8)

2. 'Red Carpet' Joseph's coat (*Alternanthera ficoidea* 'Red Carpet', Zones 9-11)

3. Golden shrimp plant (*Pachystachys lutea*, Zones 10-11)

4. Shrimp plant (*Justicia brandegeana*, Zone 11)

what to do with a pot-bound plant

Whether you're potting up a new plant from the nursery or repotting an existing container plant, break up the roots of a pot-bound plant by whatever means necessary. This might mean gently teasing the roots loose, ripping them apart with your hands, or slicing into the root mass with a knife or shovel. Roots are tougher than you might think, so don't be afraid to get rough with them. Until you convince girdled roots that they have room to spread out and grow, they will continue thinking that they're in the pot and will strangle the plant.

The foliage of these two plants varies dramatically in terms of shape and habit. The Dragon Wing® begonia has a rangy habit with thin, ovate, curled leaves, while the Lemon Coral™ sedum is short, stocky, and upright in habit with narrow, needle-like leaves.

TOP LEFT Flowers have texture, too. The red, fuzzy flowers of 'New Look' cockscomb are a classic example. This container also flaunts the dramatic variegated foliage of Painted Paradise™ Pink Improved New Guinea impatiens and 'Tricolor' St. John's wort. The flowers of 'Bright Eyes' crocosmia float above the composition.

ABOVE Leaf surfaces vary greatly in texture. Here, the elephant's ears have a soft, matte finish, while the begonia is bumpy to touch, and the wire vine has a glossy surface.

LEFT This container combination begs to be touched. It features the silky soft flowers of 'Royal Velvet' petunia and the rough, wrinkled leaves of 'Marine' heliotrope.

a tactile composition

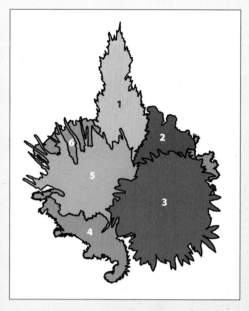

1. 'Wilma Goldcrest' Monterey cypress (*Cupressus macrocarpa* 'Wilma Goldcrest', Zones 7-11)

2. Two-row sedum (*Sedum spurium* cv., Zone 4-9)

3. 'Rudolph' wood spurge (*Euphorbia* x *martinii* 'Rudolph', Zones 7-10)

4. 'Angelina' sedum (*Sedum rupestre* 'Angelina', Zones 6-9)

5. Scotch heather (*Calluna vulgaris* cv., Zones 4-7)

6. October daphne (*Sedum sieboldii,* Zones 6-9)

• balance

While balance is an important consideration in any garden design, it is often given even more attention when designing containers and placing them in the landscape. Balance can be symmetric, as with paired pots on either side of an entry. It can also be asymmetric, as in the clustering of several pots to anchor a corner of a patio. Balance is especially important when creating a multiplant combination in a single pot to serve as the focal point in a garden or landscape. While the balance may be either symmetric or asymmetric, depending upon the garden style, plantings that call attention to themselves benefit from a sense of stability. You don't want a pot that feels like it wants to tip over.

Balance can refer to the way a pot is planted or the way containers are arranged. Here, matching planters with bay laurel underplanted with variegated Algerian ivy provide a balanced focal point marking the entry to this traditional home. The smaller pots contain standard gardenias and maidenhair ferns.

EYE-CATCHING COMBINATIONS

1. Red mistletoe cactus (*Pseudorhipsalis ramulosa*, Zone 11)

2. Diamond Frost® euphorbia (*Euphorbia* 'Inneuphdia', Zones 10-11)

3. 'Lemon & Lime' coleus (*Solenostemon scutellarioides* 'Lemon & Lime', Zone 11)

•color

Everyone loves color in the landscape, even if they have a preference for greens and whites or other subtle hues. But containers offer an especially easy way to introduce bold spots of bright color. That's because annuals and tropical plants, both known for their bright and varied colors, are ideally suited to containers. Annuals are simply tossed at the end of the season, and tropicals can either be replaced or overwintered indoors. Color schemes can be complementary (contrasting) or harmonious in nature and easily tied to the color of the containers, if desired. Bright colors used in containers also offer a great way to draw the eye through the landscape—white, red, and electric colors will be the first to grab anyone's attention.

ABOVE Tropical plants aren't the only ones to flaunt colorful foliage. This collection of shade-lovers is proof positive. Geraniums, coral bells, and hellebores are showcased in many shades of green, blue, yellow, and burgundy.

LEFT This flaming composition highlights shades of burgundy, yellow, and green in a range of leaves. All of the colors found in the 'Sky Fire' coleus, 'Lemon Twist' plectranthus, and 'Blackie' sweet potato vine can also be found in the bold leaves of Tropicanna® canna.

loose symmetry in a single pot

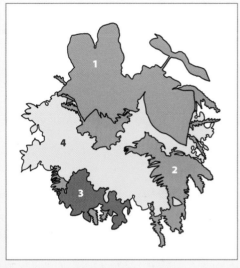

1. 'Red Flash' caladium
   (*Caladium bicolor* 'Red
   Flash', Zones 10-11)

2. 'Rita's Gold' Boston fern
   (*Nephrolepis exaltata* 'Rita's
   Gold', Zones 10-11)

3. 'Troy's Gold' plectranthus
   (*Pectranthus ciliatus* 'Troy's
   Gold', Zones 10-11)

4. Dazzler™ Mix impatiens
   (*Impatiens walleriana*
   Dazzler™ Mix, annual)

combining color contrasts and harmonies

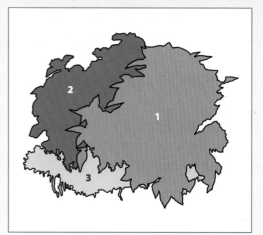

1. 'The Line' coleus (*Solenostemon scutellarioides* 'The Line', Zone 11)

2. 'Dark Star' coleus (*Solenostemon scutellarioides* 'Dark Star', Zone 11)

3. 'Angel Mist Purple' angelonia (*Angelonia* 'Angel Mist Purple', annual)

ABOVE Start with an unusual color to create an especially eye-catching composition. The 'Maori Maiden' New Zealand flax accomplishes that for this composition. Filling in and complementing the flax are a spotted coleus and burgundy-leaved 'Concorde' Japanese barberry.

LEFT This designer color-coordinates everything—the plants, the pots, *and* the house. The pots, one of which was handmade, are tucked into the existing landscape almost as sculptural elements. By color-coordinating all elements, the house and garden are clearly united.

shades of green for a natural pairing

1. 'Polly' African mask (*Alocasia* x *amazonica* 'Polly', Zones 10-11)

2. 'Snow Capped' begonia (*Begonia* 'Snow Capped', Zone 11)

3. 'Winning Streak' variegated corn (*Zea mays* 'Winning Streak', annual)

4. Peacock spikemoss (*Selaginella uncinata*, Zones 6-9)

5. 'Silver Falls' dichondra (*Dichondra argentea* 'Silver Falls', Zones 10-11)

6. English ivy (*Hedera helix* cv., Zones 5-11)

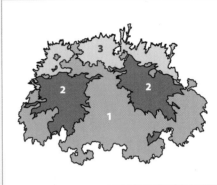

gray softens the effect

1. Avalanche™ Rose petunia (*Petunia* Avalanche™ Rose, annual)

2. 'Sweet Caroline Bewitched Purple' sweet potato vine (*Ipomoea batatas* 'Sweet Caroline Bewitched Purple', Zone 11)

3. Dusty miller (*Senecia cineraria*, Zones 8-11)

A single plant, like this 'Partytime' alternanthera, can make a colorful splash all on its own. It appreciates afternoon shade, so it's a great plant for brightening darker corners of the garden.

RIGHT Tinges of deep burgundy pull this composition together. They can be found in the leaves of 'Trailing Burgundy' coleus, 'Chocolate Chip' bugleweed, 'Tricolor' cordyline, and 'Caramel' coral bells.

BELOW The pink flower heads of 'Bertram Anderson' sedum harmonize with the bold burgundy leaves of 'Red Threads' alternanthera to create a simple yet stunning duo. The sedum foliage is gray, which acts as a blender and adds an overall softening effect.

red, white, and green—a perennial favorite

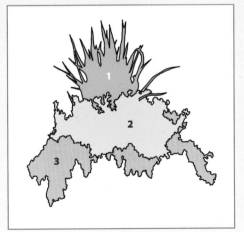

1. Japanese blood grass (*Imperata cylindrica* 'Red Baron', Zones 5-9)

2. Wink™ Garnet diascia (*Diascia* Wink™ Garnet, Zones 8-9)

3. Cascading ornamental oregano (*Origanum libanoticum,* Zones 5-10)

single pot, single plant

●●● THE EASIEST WAY TO GET STARTED WITH containers is by placing a single plant in a pot. That way, you can learn about the plant's size and growth habits, as well as move the pot about to experiment with plant combinations. But placing one plant per pot isn't just for beginners. Even the most advanced container gardeners love the flexibility offered by this strategy and often stage elaborate borders on patios and rooftops by mixing and matching single-plant container plantings—placing them at different heights on overturned pots, bricks, boxes and tables—and tucking in garden ornaments for added flair. In other words, a container garden isn't just a garden in a container—it's lots of containers used to create a garden.

Sometimes a plant just wants to be by itself and is strong enough visually to go solo. This variegated dwarf agave is a perfect example. Its bold shape, broad leaves, and yellow variegation help it stand out in the landscape.

ABOVE Single plants in pots have been highlighted individually on stands and tables, used to create a sense of repetition along the windowsill, and grouped to form a cluster of contrasting foliage and flowers.

LEFT This Dragon Wing® begonia doesn't need companions. It is a stunning specimen on its own, with attractive foliage and flowers that bloom nonstop in shade. The electric blue pot provides the perfect accent.

staged container gardens

When staging container gardens, the trick is to think about the space to be filled and not just the containers. Container plantings can be clustered to soften corners, anchor columns, and call attention to passageways. They can be set on blocks and tables or hung from walls and eaves to add an upright accent. A row of pots can create a wall between seating, cooking, and dining spaces, turning a broad terrace into a series of cozy outdoor rooms. Consider including trees and vines, or simply use big, bold plants such as bananas, as focal points to anchor your contained borders, and then surround yourself with plants, moving the pots around until they look and feel just right.

FACING PAGE Stagger the height of plants in a container garden to make it feel larger. This gardener achieved height in the back by raising pots on stands, using larger plants, and growing vines up structures.

LEFT These pots of individual plants were staged along the edge of a patio to create a bridge between the outdoor living space and landscape. Together, they form a lush, dense, and colorful border.

BELOW Place pots at ground level, clustered at grade changes, and raised on benches to vary the height of plantings and bring them closer to eye level.

overwintering tender container plants

You promised yourself that you wouldn't buy too many expensive, luscious tropicals for your container gardens this year, but it was a promise easily broken. And now you have to find a way to protect your investment and keep these treasures safe until they can return to your patio next year. Here are two ways to do it:

• Give them lots of light and heat. The best place is a warm, bright location. Before the first frost, bring them indoors and place them in front of a sunny window. You can cut the plants back by as much as two-thirds to make them more manageable. Rotate them occasionally so that they don't become misshapen from reaching for the sun. Plants that usually make attractive houseplants (such as begonias or ferns) are best suited for this treatment.

• Force them into dormancy. Many tender plants will go dormant if you place them in a cool, dark location during the winter months. Reduce your watering and fertilizing in late summer and then give them a light pruning right before the first hard frost. Drag the plants inside, and store them in a basement or unheated garage (someplace that stays chilly but won't allow them to freeze). They won't need to be watered again until you place them back outside in spring. Plants like bananas and brugmansias do well with this mode of care.

—Fine Gardening *staff*

The great thing about growing one plant in a pot is that you can move the pots around to your heart's content, changing the color combinations or moving flowering plants in and out of the picture as they come into and go out of their peak performance.

LEFT Six pots of foliage plants are clustered for a combination that begs to be touched. The variegated 'Vancouver Centennial' geranium takes center stage in this otherwise green, textural composition.

BELOW If you pack enough plants of different sizes together on a patio, you can almost duplicate the look of a lush garden border. Think like you would when designing a border, using pots of plants in multiples of three, five, or more to create bold masses of texture and color.

LEFT In informal gardens, clustered containers are generally more pleasing than rows of pots. Other ornaments, from a rabbit statuary to colorful balls to found objects, can be tucked into compositions for added interest.

BELOW Dozens of pots of foliage plants soften the architecture and surround a seating area, creating a cozy dining area just outside the kitchen door. They also provide an inviting view from the adjacent family room.

'Swane's Gold' cypress

small trees for large containers

LATIN NAME	COMMON NAME	KEY FEATURES
Acer circinatum	Vine maple	Winding branches, palmate leaves
Acer griseum	Paperbark maple	Reddish, peeling bark
Acer palmatum cvs.	Japanese maple	Spring foliage color
Chionanthus spp.	Fringe tree	Delicate, white flowers
Citrus x meyeri	Meyer lemon	Colorful, edible fruit
Corylus avellana 'Contorta'	Harry Lauder's walking stick	Contorted branches
Cryptomeria japonica 'Elegans'	Japanese cedar	Feathery, evergreen foliage
Cupressus sempervirens 'Swane's Gold'	Golden cypress	Narrowly upright with evergreen foliage
Magnolia grandiflora 'Little Gem'	Dwarf magnolia	Glossy, evergreen foliage
Pinus mugo	Mugo pine	Needled, evergreen foliage

FACING PAGE With the exception of the under-planted banana, most of the containers on this patio are planted in single pots and arranged to create a jungle-like atmosphere. Bold, tropical plants and hot colors add to the tropical impression.

ABOVE To create a special color theme for your garden, paint your furniture a favorite color and then surround it with pots of complementary and harmoniously colored plantings. With a can of spray paint, you can change your color scheme each year.

LEFT Gravel-and-soil-filled chimney flues of different heights double as containers for a variety of succulents that like good drainage. Because they are simply sections of pipe, they readily drain when set atop a bed of gravel in the garden. Staging them at different heights helps call attention to each individual plant.

single pot, multiple plants

●●● A SINGLE, LARGE POT WILL HOLD FAR MORE plants than you might imagine. In fact, it's surprisingly easy to pack a dozen or more plants into a big pot, window box, or hanging basket. Start with a single, bold plant—something to anchor the combination—and then tuck other trailing and billowing plants in around it. These may be several plants of the same variety, or any combination of different plants.

Play around with striking color combinations and seek out strong textural contrast in the leaves. Even if the focus is on flowers, be sure to include strong foliage plants to carry the container through the season. Also keep the container in mind: Can you build a color combination based on the pot color? Or do you prefer trailing plants to cover up a less decorative container? Creating container combinations is a perfect place to play, because unlike inground plantings, you can start over each season if you like.

Small tress underplanted by trailing or billowing plants are a classic combination strategy. Here, a crabapple is underplanted with gray helichrysum and scaevola.

1. 'Souvenir de Bonn' flowering maple (*Abutilon* 'Souvenir de Bonn', Zones 9-11)

2. 'Smallwood's Drive' coleus (*Solenostemon scutellarioides* 'Smallwood's Drive', Zone 11)

3. 'Bella Salmon Shade' flowering maple (*Abutilon* 'Bella Salmon Shade', Zones 9-11)

4. 'Galadriel' fuchsia (*Fuchsia* 'Galadriel', Zones 9-11)

5. 'Vanilla Twist' plectranthus (*Plectranthus ciliatus* 'Vanilla Twist', Zones 10-11)

6. 'Copper Glow' coleus (*Solenostemon scutellarioides* 'Copper Glow', Zone 11)

7. 'Sedona' coleus (*Solenostemon scutellarioides* 'Sedona', Zone 11)

8. Callie® Orange calibrachoa (*Calibrachoa* Callie® Orange, annual)

9. Variegated dwarf mirror plant (*Coprosma* x *kirkii* 'Variegata', Zones 8-10)

10. Scopia™ Gulliver White bacopa (*Sutera cordata* Scopia™ Gulliver White, annual)

forcing bulbs into bloom

forcing is an old trick that fools bulbs into blooming early. Buy bulbs in early fall, plant them in small pots filled with damp potting mix, wrap each pot in a clear plastic bag, and then place these outdoors in an area that will remain reliably cold for the time specified. Keep the soil moist, and then remove the bag and bring them indoors to a sunny windowsill when you see roots poking out from the pot's drainage holes. The warmth and light will encourage pale green shoots to emerge, and in a few weeks, you'll have spring flowers.

—*Mark Kane*

CROCUS
(*Crocus* spp. and cvs.)
Needs 15 weeks of cold, blooms in 2 to 3 weeks.

DAFFODILS
(*Narcissus* cvs.)
Needs 15 to 17 weeks of cold, blooms in 2 to 3 weeks.

FRITILLARIES
(*Fritillaria meleagris* and cvs.)
Needs 15 weeks of cold, blooms in 3 weeks.

GLORY OF THE SNOW
(*Chionodoxa luciliae* and cvs.)
Needs 15 weeks of cold, blooms in 2 to 3 weeks.

GRAPE HYACINTHS
(*Muscari* spp. and cvs.)
Needs 13 to 15 weeks of cold, blooms in 2 to 3 weeks.

HYACINTHS
(*Hyacinthus orientalis* cvs.)
Needs 11 to 14 weeks of cold, blooms in 2 to 3 weeks.

IRISES
(*Iris reticulata* and cvs.)
Needs 15 weeks of cold, blooms in 2 to 3 weeks.

PAPERWHITES
(*Narcissus papyraceus* and cvs.)
No cold required, blooms in 3 to 5 weeks.

SCILLAS
(*Scilla siberica* and cvs.)
Needs 15 weeks of cold, blooms in 2 to 3 weeks.

SNOWDROPS
(*Galanthus nivalis* and cvs.)
Needs 15 weeks of cold, blooms in 2 weeks.

TULIPS
(*Tulipa* cvs.)
Needs 14 to 20 weeks of cold, blooms in 2 to 3 weeks.

wild colors add flair to lush combos

1. Chinese parasol tree (*Firmiana simplex*, Zones 7-11)

2. Golden shrimp plant (*Pachystachys lutea*, Zones 10-11)

3. 'Katie' wild petunia (*Ruellia brittoniana* 'Katie', Zones 8-11)

4. 'Pride of Acadiana' Cajun hibiscus (*Hibiscus rosa-sinensis* 'Pride of Acadiana', Zone 11)

5. Golden oregano (*Origanum vulgare* 'Aureum', Zones 4-9)

Clusters of pots with succulent plants liven up a stairwell. The pots were carefully picked to subtly stand out from the stucco wall and to provide an orange and gray-green color scheme for the plantings.

canna provides a bold, upright accent

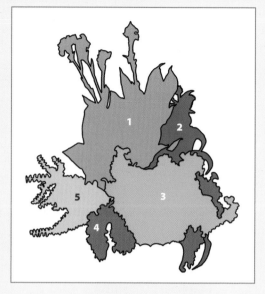

1. 'Pretoria' canna (*Canna* 'Pretoria', Zones 8-11)

2. Cardoon (*Cynara cardunculus,* Zones 7-10)

3. 'Illumination Rose' tuberous begonia (*Begonia* 'Illumination Rose', Zone 11)

4. 'Apricot Trifle' nasturtium (*Tropaeolum majus* 'Apricot Trifle', annual)

5. Silver dollar gum (*Eucalyptus cinerea,* Zones 8-10)

a cool color combo

1. Honey bush (*Melianthus major*, Zones 8-11)

2. Angelface® Wedgwood Blue summer snapdragon (*Angelonia angustifolia* 'Anwedg', annual)

3. Purple heart (*Tradescantia pallida* 'Purpurea', Zones 8-11)

4. 'Limelight' licorice plant (*Helichrysum petiolare* 'Limelight', Zones 9-11)

5. Silver sage (*Salvia argentea*, Zones 5-8)

6. Superbells® Blue calibrachoa (*Calibrachoa* Superbells® Blue, annual)

The blue blossoms of 'Rhea' mealycup sage, the azure blue of the pot, and the grayish blue foliage of 'Clear Skies' hebe and 'Silver Onion' echeveria unify this planting. The contrasting yellow of 'Sundance' Mexican orange blossom and 'Ogon' sedum brighten the composition.

•thrillers, fillers, and spillers

There is no better formula for creating a stunning mixed container planting than that of using thrillers, fillers, and spillers. Simply start with a thriller—a bold, architectural, and generally upright plant in the center of your container. Fill in around the base with mounding, billowing plants. And then tuck in a few trailing plants to spill out over the edges and cascade toward the ground. It works every time and is a great way to stay focused on what you need when you're surrounded by hundreds of exciting plants at the nursery each spring. Once you master this technique, experiment by tucking in a few additional plants for a more complex design.

Bold contrast in foliage shape and texture, contribute to the success of this container planting. The variegated spikes of mother-in-law's tongue rise above the rounded leaves of spotted leopard plant and trailing strands of peacock spikemoss.

variegated yucca is a reliable thriller

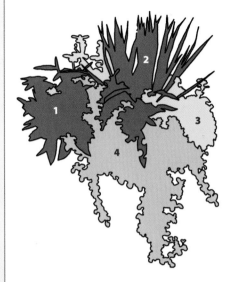

1. Purple heart (*Tradescantia pallida* 'Purple Heart', Zones 8-11)

2. Hardy yucca (*Yucca filamentosa* 'Variegata', Zones 5-10)

3. Shrubby lantana (*Lantana camara* cv., Zones 8-11)

4. 'Limelight' licorice plant (*Helichrysum petiolare* 'Limelight', Zones 9-11)

plant tightly for a lush look

regardless of the plants you select for your container garden, I recommend that you plant more closely than you would in the ground. Tight spacing makes the container look full immediately and increases the likelihood that the container will continue to look this way as the plants grow. How closely I pack them depends on the size of the plants. For example, I space annuals purchased in 4-inch nursery pots 5 to 6 inches apart and those in six-packs 1½ to 2 inches apart. In general, I try to use enough plants to conceal the edges of the container and all but hide the soil. I want the top of the container to be a vegetative tapestry from the moment I plant it.

—*Karen Kienholz Steeb*

TOP Nearly a dozen plants are packed into this tall, narrow pot. A saw palmetto provides an upright accent, while variegated St. Augustine grass trails over the edge.

RIGHT It is astounding just how many plants can be packed in a pot. This container features the varying leaf shapes and sizes of dwarf elephant's ear, orange hair sedge, golden oregano, variegated potato vine, angelonia, and lantana.

coleus both fills and spills

1. Variegated rubber plant (*Ficus elastica* 'Sylvie', Zones 10-11)

2. 'Australia' canna (*Canna* 'Australia', Zones 9-11)

3. 'Purple Emperor' coleus (*Solenostemon scutellarioides* 'Purple Emperor', Zone 11)

4. 'Molten Orange' coleus (*Solenostemon scutellarioides* 'Molten Orange', Zone 11)

5. Black-eyed cuphea (*Cuphea cyanea*, Zones 9-11)

6. Purple false eranthemum (*Pseuderanthemum atropurpureum*, Zone 11)

'Fireworks' Rex begonia

'Fishnet Stockings'

Red Abyssinian banana

bold foliage plants that thrill

LATIN NAME	COMMON NAME	KEY FEATURES
Solenostemon scutellarioides 'Fishnet Stockings'	'Fishnet Stockings' coleus	Vibrant green leaves with dark purple veins
Codiaeum cvs.	Croton	Citrus-colored variegation, waxy leaves
Isolepis cernua	Fiber-optic grass	Grows in a neat mound
Ensete ventricosum 'Maurelii'	Red Abyssinian banana	Huge plant with ruby red foliage
Alternanthera ficoidea cvs.	Joseph's coat	Thick, carpet-like growth
Alocasia and *Colocasia esculenta* cvs.	Elephant's ears	Big, floppy leaves and distinctive veins
Begonia 'Nzcone'	'Fireworks' begonia	Textured leaves, striking markings
Pennisetum purpureum 'Princess'	'Princess' napier grass	Large, sturdy grass with strappy foliage
Echeveria 'Red Glo'	'Red Glo' echeveria	Pinkish red trim, curvy form
Yucca filamentosa cvs.	Yucca	Striking variegation, interesting shape

Burgundy and yellow is a contemporary color combination that is especially popular in naturalistic gardens. This burgundy-foliaged New Zealand flax will eventually fill a pot, but colorful annuals tucked in around the base at planting time should easily last a season.

a blousy spiller adds a full skirt

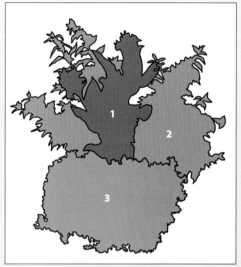

1. 'Conestoga' canna (*Canna* 'Conestoga', Zones 8-11)

2. 'Golden Edge' pigeon berry (*Duranta erecta* 'Golden Edge', Zones 9-11)

3. 'Saphira' scaevola (*Scaevola aemula* 'Saphira', Zones 10-11)

RIGHT Nursery standards like this pink geranium and spike plant can create stunning combinations. Spend an afternoon at a nursery playing around with combinations. Fill your cart with what's available and interesting, and then just start mixing and matching for serendipitous surprises.

BELOW Coleus just may be the most versatile container plant. Not only does it come in an infinite color range, but it also features a range of leaf shapes and habits, enabling you to create a pot of thrillers, fillers, and spillers just from coleus varieties.

delicate spiller softens a dramatic combo

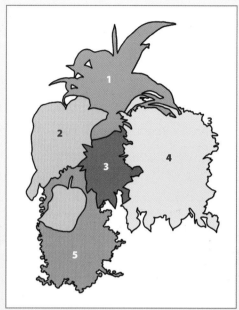

1. 'Dr. Brown' cordyline (*Cordyline fruticosa* 'Dr. Brown', Zone 11)

2. Begonia (*Begonia* cv., annual)

3. Painted Paradise™ Red New Guinea impatiens (*Impatiens walleriana* Painted Paradise™ Red, annual)

4. Dazzler™ Rose impatiens (*Impatiens walleriana* Dazzler™ Rose, annual)

5. Creeping wire vine (*Muehlenbeckia axillaris*, Zones 8-10)

specialty container plantings

3

• • •

ONE OF THE GREAT THINGS ABOUT GARDENING IS THAT IT APPEALS TO both the generalist and specialist. Some simply want a beautiful garden; others prefer collecting specialty plants or creating specific types of gardens. Container gardening is no exception. You can create great containers filled with edible fruits, vegetables, and herbs; wile away the hours trimming your topiaries; or showcase your collection of dwarf evergreens.

Some gardeners prefer certain seasons for enjoying their gardens or perhaps enjoy different parts of the landscape at different times of the year. Southerners love springtime, before the heat and humidity levels rise. Gardeners in northern climes want to make the most of every summer day. Those who enjoy their porch in spring may migrate to the pool in summer, and then to a patio or deck in the fall. Container plantings can be created to highlight each of these seasons. And every home can benefit from indoor container plantings year-round.

Although they require oversized pots, small fruit trees such as this Eureka lemon are suitable for both edible and ornamental container gardens. The lemon tree is under-planted with purple Million Bells® calibrachoa, white bacopa, and ivy.

Certain containers have unique planting or care needs, such as window boxes and hanging baskets, container water gardens, or those filled with succulents. Those that contain climbing plants benefit from the upright accent of a decorative stake, teepee, or trellis, while just about any collection of container plants can be spruced up with carefully placed decorative accents. More often than not, whatever you can do in a garden, you can do in a container garden—just on a smaller scale.

succulent mosaics

●●● SUCCULENTS ARE IDEALLY SUITED TO containers. A group of plants with thick, fleshy stems and leaves that are native to arid climates, succulents can bake in the summer heat and nearly thrive on neglect. In fact, too much water can kill them, so make sure they have good drainage, sandy soil, and adequate air circulation. Unlike most plants, many succulents are perfectly suited to small or shallow pots.

Cacti, hens and chicks, echeveria, sedums, and many euphorbias are among the succulents that will grow in containers. Their leaves are highly varied in shape, texture, and color. Tuck in several together and watch them create a tapestry or mosaic in no time. While most are not hardy and can't survive harsh winters, many sedums thrive as perennials in even cold climates. Many reproduce rapidly and will quickly fill a shallow bowl.

ABOVE A small bowl of brightly colored succulents provides a focal point along a garden path and helps mark a grade change in the landscape. This bowl is filled with grassy blue fescue, purple-leaved 'Fuldaglut' sedum, and purple and blue 'Perle von Nurnberg' echeveria.

RIGHT The way these succulents grow, you would think they were planted in the garden. Yet the large, green-and-white-variegated 'Sunburst' aeonium, the hens and chicks, and the trailing, blue senecio are all planted in pots.

bold foliage stars in a succulent combination

EYE-CATCHING COMBINATIONS

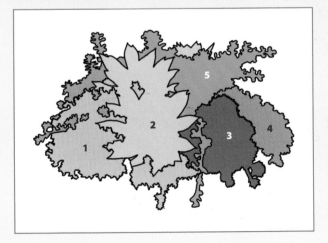

1. Sedum (*Sedum* cv., Zones 6-11)

2. Ghost plant (*Graptopetalum paraguayense*, Zone 11)

3. Hens and chicks (*Sempervivum* sp., Zones 4-11)

4. 'Ogon' sedum (*Sedum makinoi* 'Ogon', Zones 6-9)

5. Variegated mini jade plant (*Portulacaria afra* 'Variegata', Zones 10-11)

RIGHT These succulent- and ivy-filled containers are actually part of a "green" retaining wall system. Such low-maintenance plants are ideal for creating green walls that require minimal care.

BELOW This concrete basket is filled with an assortment of green-and-purple-foliaged hens and chicks. They get their name from the mother plant, or hen, which reproduces rapidly and has lots of small offspring, or chicks.

a textural tabletop mosaic

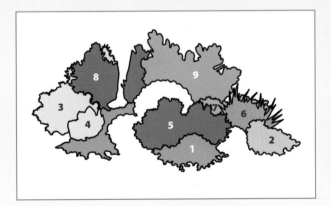

1. 'Elfin' thyme (*Thymus serphyllum* 'Elfin', Zones 4-9)

2. Creeping sedum (*Sedum grisebachii*, Zones 5-9)

3. 'Angelina' sedum (*Sedum rupestre* 'Angelina', Zones 6-9)

4. 'Silver Spoons' echeveria (*Echeveria* 'Silver Spoons', Zone 11)

5. Coppertone sedum (*Sedum nussbaumerianum*, Zones 10-11)

6. Haworthia (*Haworthia attenuata*, Zone 11)

7. 'Ogon' sedum (*Sedum makinoi* 'Ogon', Zones 6-9)

8. Baby jade plant (*Crassula ovata arborescens* 'Baby Jade', Zones 9-11)

9. Dwarf crassula (*Crassula* sp., Zone 11)

topiaries

●●● TOPIARIES ARE PLANTS THAT HAVE BEEN clipped and trained into unique shapes. It takes patience and attention to detail to grow topiaries, but they provide a perfect centerpiece for a table, make a formal statement flanking either side of a front door, and add an element of whimsy to container gardens. Traditionally, topiaries were primarily clipped shrubs and trees. Over the years, many herbs such as rosemary and germander have proven suitable as well, and these are both faster growing and more forgiving to wayward pruners than shrubs and trees. Another type of topiary is a wire-frame structure filled with damp sphagnum moss and planted with little-leaved creepers such as woolly thyme, Corsican mint, duckfoot ivy, creeping fig, wire vine, or baby's tears. For a head start, purchase established topiaries at a nursery and simply focus on maintaining them, as they'll need ongoing attention above and beyond watering.

Creeping fig topiaries like this one are created by planting small plugs of creeping fig directly in damp sphagnum moss, which fills a wire frame. When the moss feels dry to the touch, it's time to water.

fertilizing containers

fertilizing goes hand in hand with watering and can be done at the same time. Feeding potted plants is essential to replace the nutrients that leach away during daily waterings. During the growing season, add a tablespoon of water-soluble fertilizer to each gallon of water every 10 days to 2 weeks. In the fall, when plant growth slows, you can cut back on the frequency.

—*Sydney Eddison*

Spiral topiaries begin their lives as cone-shaped, evergreen shrubs or small trees, which are then tediously shaped. Here, a blue juniper has been trimmed into a swirling tower of needled foliage.

Germander is an excellent choice for this herbal standard, as it has a woody stem and bushy growth that can be trimmed easily. Patience is required, as the plant may need a season or two of growth before it is fully formed and sizeable.

structures for containers

●●● OBELISKS, STAKES, FRAMES, TEEPEES, and trellises are just as suitable for containers as they are for gardens. They can provide support for tall plants like lilies, which tend to topple in a breeze, or for edibles, which would otherwise droop from the weight of their fruit. They are also ideal for climbing and clambering plants, from rambling roses and delicate clematis vines to pole beans and fragrant jasmine.

Match the type of climber to the right type of structure. Vines climb by twining themselves around a stake, by attaching themselves directly to a flat surface with clinging roots, or with petioles and tendrils that need something to grasp. Tomatoes appreciate supports to rest their branches on, and tall, wispy plants may need to be tied to stakes. When selecting plants, remember that many vines will stretch far beyond the container and its supports, so either stick with smaller varieties or place the pots with structures next to architectural elements, such as posts or arbors, so climbers can continue on their way.

FAR RIGHT A wooden obelisk provides support for a fragrant jasmine vine and adds a note of formality to the landscape. Containers with fragrant flowers should be placed where they will be passed frequently or even lightly brushed against.

RIGHT An expandable bamboo teepee provides support for Japanese eggplant, which will bear heavy fruit later in the season. This edible planting also features Italian parsley, chives, and 'Siam Queen' basil.

bamboo stakes support an edible

1. 'Mandarin' bell pepper (*Capsicum annuum* 'Mandarin', annual)

2. 'Explosive Ember' ornamental pepper (*Capsicum annuum* 'Explosive Ember', annual)

3. Mexican feather grass (*Stipa tenuissima*, Zones 7-11)

ornamented container gardens

●●● IT'S JUST AS MUCH FUN TO TUCK ornaments into container plantings as it is into a garden bed or border. Sculptural objects of all kinds, especially those mounted on the end of a small stake, are easy to add to any container garden. Some of them can even double as stakes for plants that need a little support. For larger containers, consider working in one or more colorful ceramic or glass balls, which can quickly pull together a color scheme. Old gardening hand tools and random found objects make wonderful conversation pieces, and decorative plant labels can be as interesting as they are informative. Simply take them into account when designing your container, thinking of their contribution to form, color, and texture just as you would if you were adding another plant.

Every garden needs a cat. This one not only eavesdrops on conversations, but also guards pots of New Zealand flax, plectranthus, Japanese forest grass, and succulents with a stern attitude and never fails to make garden visitors laugh.

ABOVE Bocce balls add a smooth, spherical element to a window box that is covered in a mass of textural baby's tears. Annual pink impatiens add a spot of color to the otherwise very simple planting.

LEFT Antique or castaway gardening tools can add interesting accents to containers. An old, rusted hand trowel provides contrasting colors and textures to this composition and serves as a conversation starter.

window boxes

●●● WINDOW BOXES, ALSO KNOWN AS WINDOW baskets, hayracks, and flower troughs, are a great way to add architectural interest to a house as well as lush foliage and flowers to outdoor spaces. And one of the best things about them is that they are often at or above eye level, hanging not only beneath first- and second-floor windows but also from balconies and decks.

Because of their location, window boxes can be a challenge to maintain and freshen up. Consider window box liners, which are inserts that can be preplanted and slipped directly into an existing window box with ease. It's a great way to update window boxes annually or by season. Predrilled window boxes make hanging easier. And self-watering window boxes, which have water reservoirs, greatly simplify daily chores, as these types of containers tend to dry out quickly and easily, especially when placed in full sun and exposed to wind. While they may require a bit more upkeep, window boxes add so much personality to a home that they are worth the extra effort.

securing and planting a window box

unless your design inspiration is the Leaning Tower of Pisa, you should do a little planning before going gung ho with your window box planting. Follow these recommendations to make your weekend do-it-yourself project go a little easier:

- Measure, measure, measure. Position your box before drilling. Measure the center of the box and the center of the window for your first hole. Position additional bolts about every foot to provide enough support.
- Use lag bolts (thick screws that don't bend) to mount the box to your house.
- Consider installing drip irrigation in your window boxes to cut down on watering hassles.
- Choose plants that fit the conditions. If your site is shady, you don't want plants that need full sun.

—Fine Gardening *editors*

FACING PAGE This window box is packed with plants. Cardoon plays a starring role and is surrounded by setcrecea, Makinoi sedum, burro's tail sedum, Diamond Frost® euphorbia, angelonia, and shrimp plant.

TOP A colorful and formal window box dresses up the front of an in-town cottage. The clipped dwarf-boxwood standards create a sense of unity by echoing the shape of boxwoods planted along the foundation and throughout the garden.

LEFT Window boxes enliven a narrow side-yard passageway that leads to a backyard garden. Each window box is planted differently, with a range of plants including green and variegated ivies, ornamental grasses, and even edible Swiss chard.

hanging baskets

●●● LIKE OTHER CONTAINERS, HANGING baskets may be filled with a single plant or many. They also come in a range of shapes and sizes that can be hung from above or from the side. Traditional hanging baskets are those solid containers in which the top is planted with trailing plants that spill over the edges. However, an open-sided basket filled with a permeable liner allows three to four times the number of plants to be planted in staggered rows on all sides in addition to the top, creating a larger mass and greater variety in color, texture, and visual interest. Also, keep in mind that hanging baskets aren't just for flowers. Succulents, ornamental grasses, ferns, and even trailing tomatoes can spice up plantings.

Liner choices include sphagnum moss, coco fiber, burlap, and synthetic materials. The bigger the basket, the less often they'll need to be watered. Just remember that large baskets packed with plants and soil can be very heavy when watered, so make sure all beams or eaves and hardware can support them.

Colorful lobelia, calibrachoa, and strawflower are packed into a simple hanging basket, providing a touch of rustic charm to this shed door.

ABOVE This cone-shaped hanging basket is lined with a plastic liner to help prolong the life of the basket. It is top-planted with trailing variegated ivy, pansies, and a dwarf evergreen.

LEFT Held by a sturdy iron bracket, this hanging basket was designed with thrillers, fillers, and spillers in mind—the upright spikes of cordyline, billowing pansy flowers, and trailing ivy.

container water gardens

●●● CONTAINER WATER GARDENS ARE A wonderfully easy way to bring the joy of water gardening to any outdoor space. Start with a waterproof basin—anything that holds water and is large enough for plants will do. Plug and seal any holes. Porous pots can be glazed with a waterproof sealer on the inside.

Fill your container with water and plants that love wet feet—those that naturally grow in bogs and directly in water—staging the pots on bricks or overturned empty pots as needed. Moisture-loving plants that grow in soil should be planted in their own container with heavy, claylike soil and then placed in the water basin. Design as you would any container garden: For multiple water plants in a single pot, seek out a mix of those with an upright accent, a billowing nature, and a trailing or floating habit.

Diminutive duckweed fills a pot of water that has been tucked in among shrubs and perennials in a garden border. This tiny, floating plant spreads rapidly and grows in dense colonies, making it ideal for a container but potentially invasive in the wild.

Horsetail, with its segmented spires, loves wet feet and will grow in pots of damp soil. The pot is placed in a saucer so that the roots have continuous access to moisture. It can also be placed in a pond.

A dwarf gunnera grows in a gravel-and-water-filled concrete container. Its masses of heart-shaped leaves add textural contrast to the surrounding hillside garden. This entire garden is composed of foliage for a tapestry-like effect.

soil for aquatic plants

W hen it comes to choosing the best potting mix for aquatic plants, there is no one right answer. Ideally, it should supply anchorage, fertilization, and moisture retention. It should also be easy to use, odorless, and not make the water look muddy. Do not choose traditional potting soil, as the organic matter will decompose, releasing salts and other substances that may burn plant roots. Lighter-weight potting soil ingredients such as perlite and vermiculite will also float to the top of your container. Here are five alternate choices.

• **Clay soil** holds water and nutrients and effectively anchors plants. However, it can muddy the water if disturbed often.

• **Cat litter** isn't a potting medium but it works well as one. Litter made from calcified clay is best because it has not been chemically treated or deodorized. It holds nutrients and moisture, yet won't muddy the water. It also does not float or clump.

• **Pebbles and pea gravel** are ideal for filtration plants—such as rushes, reeds, and pickerelweeds—whose roots can catch nutrients as they pass through the water.

• **Coco fiber** is also good for filtration plants. Because it is much lighter than gravel, however, top-heavy plants may fall over.

• **Sand** is good for short plants with creeping habits. However, sand does not hold nutrients, so plants should be fertilized regularly.

—*Greg Speichert*

TOP Pots of carnivorous pitcher plants are placed directly in a shallow section of a backyard pond. In the wild, these plants grow in damp bogs and shallow standing water. Many produce a nectar that is irresistible to wasps and yellow jackets.

ABOVE The broad, round leaves of lotus dance in the air like small umbrellas. Tucked into a perennial border, this container planting becomes a focal point in the garden.

FACING PAGE This lightweight resin pot is home to elephant's ears, dwarf papyrus, and parrot's feather. It is a focal point on a partially shaded wooden deck and is surrounded by a variety of nonwater plants.

'Black Magic' elephant's ears

Napoleon™ papyrus

plants that like wet feet

W hile most water garden plants grow in soil, they don't mind having wet feet. Indeed, most thrive with their roots saturated on a consistent basis. Certain aquatic plants tend to be invasive in certain parts of the country if released into the wild, so play it safe and make sure that you keep these contained.

LATIN NAME	COMMON NAME	KEY FEATURES
Nelumbo 'Momo Botan'	Dwarf lotus	Deep, rosy red, double flowers
Nymphaea cvs.	Water lilies	Day- or night-blooming, floating flowers
Typha laxmannii 'Europa'	Dwarf cattail	Graceful spires of brown flowers that look like sausage links
Cyperus papyrus Napoleon™	Papyrus	Architecturally upright, spiky foliage, bell-shaped flower clusters
Acorus calamus	Sweet flag	Grassy, iris-like foliage
Myriophyllum aquaticum	Parrot feather	Soft, feathery tufts of foliage
Sagittaria latifolia	Duck potato	Arrowhead-shaped leaves and white flowers
Houttuynia cordata 'Chameleon'	Chameleon plant	Red-, green-, and cream-variegated foliage
Hymenocallis caribaea 'Variegata'	Variegated spider lily	Electric, variegated, green-and-white leaves
Sarracenia flava	Yellow pitcher plant	Erect, trumpet-shaped, insect-eating leaves

RELIABLE PLANT PICKS

In a container garden, it is possible to place plants with dramatically different cultural needs side by side. The agave and barrel cactus need dry, well-drained soil, while the rush in the adjacent pot is perfectly content in standing water.

edible container gardens

●●● WHAT COULD BE BETTER THAN PICKING fresh herbs and vegetables just outside your back door? Most culinary herbs and edible flowers, and even many fruits and vegetables, are ideal for growing in containers. Look for compact and bushing varieties of vegetables and provide cages, stakes, and other support structures for those with vining habits or heavy fruits. Larger, sprawling vegetables such as squashes need barrels and large containers. Herbs, radishes, lettuces, and other edibles with compact root systems will do well in modestly sized pots and window boxes. Most root vegetables, such as carrots, parsnips, and potatoes, need deep pots; the exception is radishes, which are fine in shallower pots. Vegetables and fruits must be fertilized frequently (approximately every three weeks with a liquid fertilizer). Most herbs are fine with little or no fertilization.

The pinkish flowers of variegated society garlic dance above the pungent foliage of purple sage, while pots of fragrant rosemary sit nearby. All can be used in cooking.

A pungent and prostrate rosemary spills from a chimney flue, which easily doubles as a container when set upright and filled with soil. Rosemary needs good drainage, but you don't want it to dry out.

a juicy combination

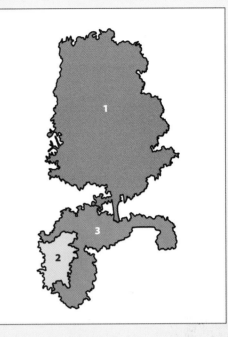

1. 'Dancy' mandarin orange (*Citrus reticulata* 'Dancy', Zones 9-11)

2. Million Bells® calibrachoa (*Calibrachoa* Million Bells®, Zones 9-11)

3. Blue petunia (*Petunia* cv., annual)

Pansies

Garland chrysanthemum

a bouquet of edible flowers

edible flowers add an unexpected accent to many dishes. Sprinkle them over salads, stir them into drinks, use them when making jams and jellies, or steep them in oils and vinegars for added flavor.

LATIN NAME	COMMON NAME	KEY FEATURES
Taraxacum officinale	Dandelion	Yellow flowers eaten fresh or used in wine
Viola x *wittrockiana* cvs.	Pansies	Colorful garnish with mild, minty flavor
Mentha spp. and cvs.	Mints	Use liberally in Middle Eastern dishes and mojitos
Cucurbita pepo cvs.	Squash and pumpkin	Stuff with herbal cheese and deep fry
Chrysanthemum coronarium	Garland chrysanthemum	Delicious in salads and Asian dishes

ABOVE This window box includes a variety of mints and alpine strawberries. The plants are closely packed and harvested as needed for cooking and to keep the plants compact.

RIGHT This deep raised-bed-style box planter has space for a mix of bushy and sprawling herbs, including sages, sweet lavender, French lavender, thymes, sweet marjoram, winter savory, oregano, and rosemaries.

Chile peppers are warm-season crops that grow happily in pots. The drier, hotter, and sunnier the conditions, the hotter the peppers become. Shown here (clockwise from center back) are 'Rojo Morado', 'Fresno', 'Orange Blossom', 'Magenta', 'Hot Claw', 'Royal Black', and 'Dog Bite'.

ABOVE Sweet bay is a favorite seasoning for soups and stews and is well-suited to container culture in warmer climates. It is a sturdy, slow-growing, shrub-like tree that retains its leaves in winter.

RIGHT Inside a sunny northern California courtyard, this tangerine receives plenty of warmth from both the sun and heat radiating from the walls. The walls also provide protection from drying winds.

'Orange Blossom'

'Poinsettia'

pick a peck of chile peppers

the best peppers for pots have a compact habit, attractive foliage, and an abundance of small, colorful fruits. These ornamental types often lack the subtle flavors, but not the fire, of larger-pod types. It is best to grow the big boys in the open field because they perform poorly in pots. Here are a few favorites for ornamental use.

—Andy Goldman

LATIN NAME	KEY FEATURES
Capsicum 'Bouquet'	Purple flowers, foliage and fruits that turn red
C. 'Chinese Multicolor'	Cone-shaped pods of many colors on a large plant
C. 'Color Guard'	Upright, tapered fruits that turn from orange to purple to red
C. 'Fips'	Dwarf plant with clusters of colorful fruits.
C. 'Fresno'	Medium-hot with 3-inch-long fruits
C. 'Goat Horn'	Cayenne pepper with long pods
C. 'Marbles'	Colorful marble-sized red fruits
C. 'Orange Blossom'	Short, bushy plant with orange, erect peppers
C. 'Nosegay'	Diminutive plant loaded with small, colorful, round fruits
C. 'Poinsettia'	Clusters of upright, red peppers on compact plants
C. 'Riot'	Short, bushy plant with long, yellow pods that turn red
C. 'Rojo Morado'	Tall, elegant plant with purple flowers and fruits that turn red
C. 'Royal Black'	Tall plant with variegated foliage and small purple fruits

edibles are heavy feeders

We think of edibles as providing nutrition, but *they* need nutrition too. Fruits and vegetables are heavy feeders, so you'll need to amend your potting soil with compost and other nutrients. A standard potting mix doesn't contain enough nutrients to sustain a container full of vegetables all season long, and dousing your pots with liquid synthetic fertilizers is less than ideal because you're going to eat the contents. For a quick-fix recipe that will ensure success, mix 3 parts traditional potting soil with 1 part compost, 1 part peat moss, and a spadeful of leaf mulch. For good measure, add an occasional dose of liquid organic fertilizer to your pots.

TOP Even melons can be grown in containers. Simply start with a large container and understand that their foliage will likely wander well beyond the pot's perimeter. Like most vegetables and herbs, melons prefer full sun for six or more hours a day.

RIGHT This 'Forest Green' parsley has arching stems of tightly curled, deep green foliage that grow back quickly after being cut for cooking. A biennial that produces lots of foliage its first year, parsley flowers and dies back its second year. For generous harvests, start with new plants each spring.

1. Curly parsley (*Petroselinum crispum,* Zones 5-9)

2. Purple sage (*Salvia officinalis* 'Purpurascens', Zones 7-8)

3. Thyme (*Thymus* cv., Zones 4-10)

indoor
containers

●●● ONE OF THE HEALTHIEST THINGS YOU can do for your home is fill it with houseplants. They not only add life to a room, but they also help improve its air quality. Set indoor containers on tables, tuck them into bright corners, or place them on sunny windowsills. Arrange a cluster for impact, or combine multiple houseplants in a single pot, just as you would in an outdoor container. If you have a bright enough space, many of your summer containers can even be brought indoors to weather the winter cold, giving you a head start on the following year's outdoor garden. Don't forget that indoor plants need to be watered often, and be sure to place trays beneath your containers so that water or damp pots don't stain your floors or furniture.

ABOVE This handmade terra-cotta pot inspired a plant combination that looks like it could be found on a windswept beach. It features 'Tweed' flamingo flower, 'China Star' and 'Jade Ribbons' cast-iron plants, 'Bonnie' spider plant, 'Ellen Danica' oakleaf ivy, 'Camouflage' mother-in-law's tongue, and 'Rita's Gold' Boston fern.

RIGHT This combination delivers pattern with a punch. An old-fashioned 'Tricolor' wandering Jew anchors the planting, which also features 'Mandianum' bear's paw fern, 'Brazillian Lady' and 'Fireworks' begonias, and variegated creeping fig.

chartreuse brightens a room

1. 'Austral Gem' asplenium fern (*Asplenium* 'Austral Gem')

2. 'Florida Beauty' dracaena (*Dracaena surculos* 'Florida Beauty')

3. 'Marisela' prayer plant (*Maranta leuconeura* 'Marisela')

4. 'Golden Erubescens' philodendron (*Philodendron erubescens* 'Golden Erubescens')

5. 'Aureum' philodendron (*Philodendron scandens* 'Aureum')

seasonal plantings

• •• CONTAINER PLANTINGS MAY PEAK IN summertime, but they can add visual and textural interest to the landscape any time of the year. Consider creating seasonal plantings for the outdoor rooms you enjoy at specific times of year—such as the pool deck in summer and a sunny patio in spring—or select plants that provide season-long or even year-round interest. The secret is to think beyond flowers. Anchor a few containers with evergreen foliage that will shine in every season. And then select trees, shrubs, and perennials with multiseason interest. For instance, containers might feature spring flowers, great summer foliage, fall leaf color, and winter berries, bark, or structure. Then fill in with annuals and tropical plants for bold spots of color throughout the seasons.

ABOVE Snowdrops are among the earliest signs of spring, often flowering while there is still snow on the ground. These bulbs were potted up and clustered to create the impression of a mass planting.

RIGHT Dwarf, clipped boxwoods and trailing ivy give these containers year-round interest. Annuals can be changed out from season to season for a refreshing color scheme and to keep the planters looking healthy.

FACING PAGE The shimmering inflorescences of red fountain grass and the yellow, button-like blossoms of santolina are sure signs that summer has arrived. Spiderflower, too, is a summer favorite that grows here amid colorful foliage.

•spring

Among the quickest ways to get your containers off to a great start in spring is to focus on great foliage plants. Many perennials leaf out and grow rapidly in early spring, when temperatures are still too fickle for tender annuals, and many have excellent foliage. You can cluster pots of perennials with colorful spring annuals and dramatic tropical plants once the weather warms, or leave spots to tuck them into multiplant pots. Spring-flowering shrubs and flowering bulbs are also excellent choices for early-season containers. Plant the bulbs in fall and allow them to overwinter outdoors. Make frequent visits to nurseries in early spring, as the selection will change weekly.

TOP This box planter shows off a smart strategy for early spring. Variegated ivy gives the planting fullness, while daffodils and pansies add bright spots of color. It doesn't take many flowers to stand out against an evergreen backdrop.

RIGHT Soft-colored flowers are especially suited for spring. Compact Innocence® nemesia and violets mingle among the green, gray, and gold foliage of 'Evergold' sedge, Irish moss, wire vine, ajuga, licorice plant, and 'Citronelle' heuchera.

fragrant flowers announce spring's arrival

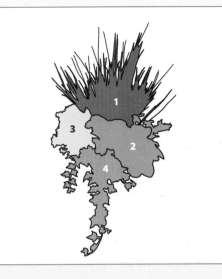

1. 'Quartz Creek' corkscrew rush (*Juncus effusus* 'Quartz Creek', Zones 4-9)

2. Cyclamen (*Cyclamen persicum* cv., annual)

3. Compact Innocence® nemesia (*Nemesia fruticans* 'Tiktoc', annual)

4. Variegated English ivy (*Hedera helix* cv., Zones 5-11)

cheerful early season companions

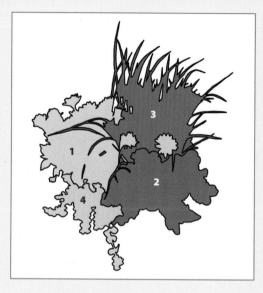

1. Soprano® Purple African daisy
    (*Osteospermum* 'Osoutis', annual)

2. Pansy (*Viola* x *wittrockiana* cv.,
    Zones 8-11)

3. 'Ogon' Japanese sweet flag
    (*Acorus gramineus* 'Ogon',
    Zones 6-9)

4. 'Goldilocks' creeping jenny
    (*Lysimachia nummularia*
    'Goldilocks', Zones 4-8)

Once the weather warms up, begonias can be moved from indoors to out to spruce up shady porches. 'Escargot' begonia has a unique leaf that contrasts dramatically with the tiny leaves of wire vine.

good-looking foliage, spring through fall

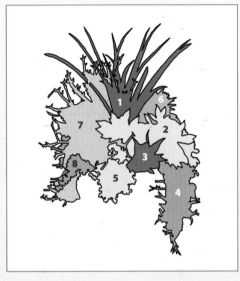

1. Ornamental pineapple (*Ananas* spp., Zones 10-11)

2. Ghost plant (*Graptopetalum paraguayense,* Zone 11)

3. 'Black Gem' aloe (*Aloe* 'Black Gem', Zones 10-11)

4. Senecio (*Senecio* sp., Zones 9-11)

5. 'Ogon' sedum (*Sedum makinoi* 'Ogon', Zones 6-9)

6. 'Golden Girl' panda plant (*Kalanchoe tomentosa* 'Golden Girl', Zone 11)

7. Pencil tree (*Euphorbia tirucalli,* Zone 11)

8. Variegated mini jade plant (*Portulacaria afra* 'Variegata', Zones 10-11)

•summer

Summer is the peak season for containers, when plantings really sizzle and shine. It's also that time of year when just about anything grows in a container—flowers, bold tropical foliage, succulents, vegetables, herbs, and more. Because there is so much to choose from, it is an excellent season to play with plant pairings by moving pots around to see what looks good together. Also, because most plants have grown closer to their mature size for the season, it's a good time to reassess combinations based on size, shape, and form. Tropical plants, which often have bold, colorful foliage and electric-colored flowers, are especially fun to play with, creating eye-catching combinations around pools and on decks and patios. Summer is a time to be adventurous.

Ornamental grasses and foliage plants like the coleus and plectranthus in this grouping really hit their stride in summer. Pruning them back by up to a third in spring will produce much fuller plants, as two new branches will emerge from each stem that was cut back.

flowers that bloom all summer long

1. 'Yellow Queen' shrimp plant (*Justicia brandegeana* 'Yellow Queen', Zones 10-11)

2. Molten Lava™ oxalis (*Oxalis vulcanicola* Molten Lava™, annual)

3. Orange hair sedge (*Carex testacea*, Zones 8-9)

4. 'Summer Candle' firecracker flower (*Crossandra infundibuliformis* 'Summer Candle', Zones 10-11)

5. Golden Mexican heather (*Cuphea hyssopifolia* 'Aurea', Zone 11)

6. Variegated vinca (*Vinca major* cv., Zones 7-9)

shrubs return summer after summer

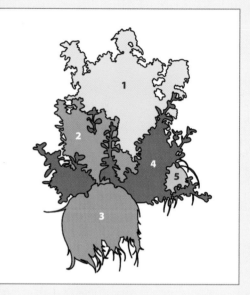

1. Sugar Tip® rose of Sharon (*Hibiscus syriacus* 'America Irene Scott', Zones 5-9)

2. Petit Bleu™ blue-mist shrub (*Caryopteris* x *clandonensis* 'Minibleu', Zones 5-9)

3. 'Amazon Mist' sedge (*Carex* 'Amazon Mist', Zones 7-10)

4. Bush germander (*Teucrium fruticans,* Zones 8-9)

5. 'Silvery Sunproof' liriope (*Liriope muscari* 'Silvery Sunproof', Zones 6-10)

ABOVE Gold and purple is a favorite summertime color combination that lasts well into fall and can be achieved by using a mix of foliage and flowers. The purple flowers of tall verbena add a nice floral accent to an otherwise foliage-dominated planting.

LEFT Place big pots out by the pool to break up large expanses of paving and to add an upright accent to an otherwise horizontal landscape. Using big pots also helps reduce watering chores in the heat of summer.

ABOVE 'Flapjack' kalanchoe looks like a summer sunset and is striking set against an evergreen background and in contrast with a smaller, low-growing sedum.

RIGHT Despite their cheery yellow flowers, the most unique feature of these nasturtiums is their round leaf. Here, 'Alaska Mix' nasturtiums harmonize with the warm hues of 'Spreading Sunset' lantana, 'Orange King' coleus, and the tall 'Louis Cotton' canna.

low-maintenance, high-impact planting

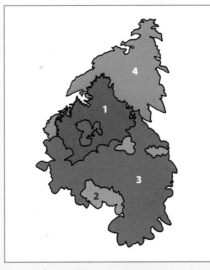

1. 'Barry's Silver' Lawson false cypress (*Chamaecyparis lawsoniana* 'Barry's Silver', Zones 5-9)

2. Cuban oregano (*Plectranthus amboinicus,* Zones 10-11)

3. 'Lemon Twist' variegated plectranthus (*Plectranthus* 'Lemon Twist', Zones 10-11)

4. 'Alabama Sunset' coleus (*Solenostemon scutellarioides* 'Alabama Sunset', Zone 11)

•fall

Cool-weather combos are the hallmark of fall. Think of plants with colorful leaves, beautiful berries, or grassy foliage. It is a time for many deciduous shrubs to shine, and small ornamental grasses can be tucked into almost any pot to replace annuals that have been frostbitten or are past their prime. Larger ornamental grasses with their showy seedheads are mainstays in many container gardens, returning each year with only minimal attention. There are also many perennials that continue to flower and put on a show in fall, making this late season just as beautiful in the container garden as it is in nature.

ABOVE Fall foliage is just as impressive in containers as it is in the garden. Here, a crabapple underplanted with cyclamen and ornamental kale.

RIGHT Chrysanthemums will always be a fall favorite. They are abundant at nurseries and garden centers and add a bold spot of color all fall long, as they do at the entry of this home.

flowering into early fall

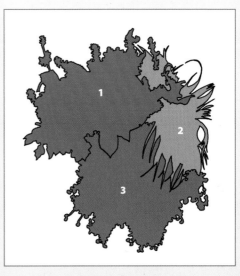

1. 'Dredge' plectranthus (*Plectranthus ciliatus* 'Dredge', annual)

2. Orange hair sedge (*Carex testacea*, Zones 8-9)

3. Creeping wire vine (*Muehlenbeckia axillaris*, Zones 8-10)

yellow is an autumn favorite

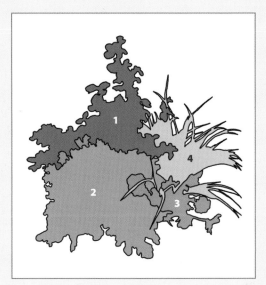

1. 'Raulston's Gold' wintercreeper (*Euonymus fortunei* 'Raulston's Gold', Zones 5-9)

2. 'Alabama Sunrise' heucherella (x *Heucherella* 'Alabama Sunrise', Zones 4-9)

3. Panola™ Primrose pansy (*Viola* x *wittrockiana* Panola™ Primrose, Zones 8-11)

4. 'Ogon' Japanese sweet flag (*Acorus gramineus* 'Ogon', Zones 6–9)

ABOVE Rather than just potting up single chrysanthemums, combine them with grasses and other flowers. Here, 'Seizan' chrysanthemum is accompanied by lemongrass, 'Frosted Curls' sedge, and pansies.

LEFT Ornamental kale makes a bold statement in cool-weather gardens. It is easy to grow, offers a bright accent of color, is rarely bothered by pests, and can even be eaten. Plant it in fall and it will last through early spring.

• winter

While the plant palette may be limited for winter, container plantings play a key role in many winter gardens. Start with a frost-proof pot—those made from structural foam and fiberglass are excellent insulating choices, while concrete and cast-stone containers are classics, and thick-walled ceramic pots are an alternative in moderate climates. Select hardy plants with winter interest—evergreen groundcovers, shrubs, and small trees are excellent choices, as are deciduous trees and shrubs with bright berries, colorful stems, or peeling bark.

If possible, give your winter containers some protection from drying winter winds. North-facing exposures, because they experience less-extreme temperature swings over the course of a day than southern and eastern exposures, provide some protection from damaging freeze-thaw cycles. Also, keep in mind that plants still must be watered in winter if Mother Nature doesn't take care of this for you. If the soil feels dry, give plants a drink of cold water when air temperatures rise above 40 degrees.

ABOVE Variegated ivies are excellent container companions for dark evergreen shrubs such as juniper. Their white or yellow variegation adds a bright accent to the winter landscape.

RIGHT Frasier firs in pots flank either side of a front door to create a welcoming entry even on snowy winter days.

evergreens anchor a winter container

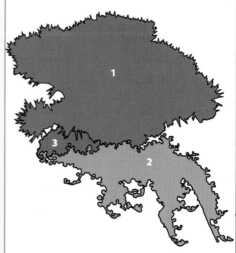

1. Mugo pine (*Pinus mugo*, Zones 3-7)

2. Creeping wire vine (*Muehlenbeckia axillaris*, Zones 8-10)

3. Twiggy spikemoss (*Selaginella sanguinolenta* var. *compressa*, Zones 6-8)

placing pots in the landscape

● ● ●

CONTAINERS ARE A WELCOME ADDITION TO EVERY PART OF THE
landscape, from driveway entries and parking courts to front porches, back stoops,
decks and patios, pathways, and gardens. With or without plants, pots can make a
strong impression—drawing attention to an area, screening unwanted views,
breaking up space, creating a welcoming environment, and shaping outdoor rooms.

With their ease of portability, container plantings can be placed throughout the
garden and landscape to address both short- and long-term needs, whether a pair of
boxwoods in classic box planters flanking either side of a doorway or a pot of colorful
annuals tucked into a temporary bare spot in a border. Containers can add a splash
of color around a pool, create visual interest wherever you gather with friends and
family, and soften the hard surfaces of a deck or patio.

Use pots as focal points in a formal garden room, courtyard, garden border, or
any place you wish to draw the eye. You can also pack staged containers together
tightly to create the impression of a generous garden border—
even where there's no ground for planting.

**Even without plants,
an attractive and
well-placed pot
like this one can
look great in the
landscape. The
key is placing pots
strategically to
serve as sculptural
focal points.**

ABOVE Although an adobe wall needs no embellishment, it shows off plants and objets d'art to perfection. Here, blue wooden pot supports make a stunning contrast to the earth-colored wall.

TOP LEFT The loose, naturalistic plantings in these pots provide a visual connection to the grassy pots on the deck as well as to a meadow-like garden on the opposite side of the pool. The big pots are also in scale with the larger pool and open landscape.

ABOVE Bold container plantings help create a warm and enticing entry. A cluster of containers with hostas and Algerian ivies, including one with a bay laurel, calls attention to the front door of this traditional home.

Agave

plant picks for focal points

S ome plants demand a starring role, which makes them ideal choices for containers that serve as focal points throughout the landscape. These plants often have an upright habit and bold, long-season foliage.

LATIN NAME	COMMON NAME	KEY FEATURES
Agapanthus cvs.	African blue lily	Thick, strappy foliage and large, rounded flower heads
Acer palmatum cvs.	Japanese maple	Small tree with interesting structure and beautiful leaves
Agave spp. and cvs.	Agave	Striking succulent foliage, sometimes variegated, with sharp thorns
Colocasia esculenta	Taro	Large, floppy leaves
Cyathea cooperi	Australian tree fern	Large, hairy fern with lush foliage
Cyperus papyrus 'Nanus'	Dwarf papyrus	Spiky flower heads atop tall green stems
Ensete ventricosum	Abyssinian banana	Tall plant with large, red-veined leaves
Eucomis comosa	Pineapple lily	Bold, fleshy foliage and a dramatic spired flower head
Miscanthus sinensis and cvs.	Eulalia grass	Bold, upright ornamental grass that shimmers in sunlight
Pennisetum setaceum 'Rubrum'	Purple fountain grass	Medium-sized grass with red foliage and swaying seed heads
Phormium tenax cvs.	New Zealand flax	Large, strappy, and colorful foliage

entries and passageways

●●● WHETHER AN INFORMAL CLUSTER OF loose, grassy plantings or a pair of matching tiered topiaries, container plantings offer an easy way to create a welcoming entry to your home, signaling to guests that you're glad they've arrived. Setting pots on either side of the door is just one way to create an exciting entry. Also consider placing pots on steps, along a path to the front door, beneath a lamppost, or in an entry garden. Choose containers that complement the style and period of your home. And plant them in such a way that they settle comfortably into your home's landscape.

Containers can also be used to highlight other passageways—whether a gate or arbor leading to another part of the landscape, a path winding through a garden, or the transition from one outdoor room to another. Place them at bends in the path or as focal points to lead the way. They can also brighten breezeways leading between your house and garage or mark the point where your driveway meets the street.

Entries include more than front doors. Here, large pots of agapanthus sit atop posts marking the street-side driveway entry for a residence. They add a soft, colorful accent to an otherwise evergreen landscape.

ABOVE This simple yet colorful container of duckweed doubles as a safety feature, calling attention to steps and marking a transitional point in the garden. The burgundy and green colors are echoed along this garden path.

LEFT This recessed residential entrance is compelling thanks to the matching topiary planters that help frame the front door and create a cozy space for guests to await entry. Daffodils add a splash of early spring color to the containers.

RIGHT Containers don't have to be updated annually. The junipers that flank this entry were planted in the 1920s. Over the years, they have been pruned into bonsai-like forms.

ABOVE Topiaries add a touch of formality wherever they are placed, making them especially appropriate for front entries, which is the most formal spot in most landscapes. They can flank a front door or be placed at the bottom of a staircase, as this one was.

RIGHT Piers and posts are perfect places for pots, bringing container plantings closer to eye level. This packed pot is anchored by an exuberant elephant's ear and softened with trailing grasses and perennials.

give backyard entries some foliage power

1. Creeping wire vine (*Muehlenbeckia axillaris,* Zones 8-10)

2. Silver sage (*Salvia argentea,* Zones 5-8)

3. 'Elijah Blue' blue fescue (*Festuca glauca* 'Elijah Blue', Zones 4-8)

4. Red chicken gizzard iresine (*Iresine herbstii,* annual)

5. Persian shield (*Strobilanthes dyerianus,* Zones 9-11)

6. 'Saturn' coleus (*Solenostemon scutellarioides* 'Saturn', Zone 11)

7. 'Crystal Palace Gem' geranium (*Perlargonium* 'Crystal Palace Gem', annual)

8. Variegated Saint Augustine grass (*Stenotaphrum secudatum* 'Variegatum', Zones 9-11)

9. Pencil cactus (*Euphorbia tirucalli,* Zones 9-11)

•entries

Whether classically or creatively planted, containers on a front porch give guests something to enjoy while they wait at the door. Formal plantings certainly suit a traditional home, but something unexpected or fragrant can provide a wonderful conversation starter. Because entry plantings make such a strong first impression, seek out tried-and-true plants with long-season good looks—those plants you've already tested and know are star performers. And think beyond the doorway, utilizing the full porch, stoop, steps, and pathway leading to the entry. Eye-catching containers strategically placed along a front path show guests which way to go and make the passage an enjoyable one. If you have a lamppost, consider planting a vine in a container that can scramble up the post.

Narrow, upright plants at the entry of a modestly sized suburban home have a visual effect that is similar to that of columns on a much larger house. The yellow-variegated snake plants in these pots are both dramatic and low-maintenance, making them ideal for containers.

freshen up pots in fall

if an arrangement looks a little ragged, I'll separate all of the components to decide which plants look healthy enough to use in new combinations. The plants I reuse have had a season to grow, which ensures that my new creations will look full right from the start. With spent annuals removed and the soil freshened up, I'm ready to transform both old and new plants into stunning fall and winter arrangements. I'll sometimes simply pot up a single large specimen that I've pulled from an old container.

—Rita Randolph

TOP Evergreens are an excellent choice for front entry plantings, as they provide year-round appeal. After all, guests continue to arrive at the front door even after the garden has gone dormant.

ABOVE Clusters of container plantings, along with a hanging basket, give this townhome its quaint, cottage-like appeal. Rambling roses add a splash of color and informality to the setting.

The solid, reassuring presence of topiary standards flanking an entryway lends a calming, timeless feel to this traditional home. A pair of matching containers add a more formal flair than a single pot placed asymmetrically would.

eden at your doorstep

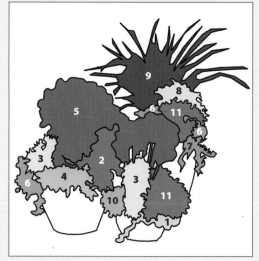

1. Creeping wire vine (*Muehlenbeckia axillaris,* Zones 8-10)

2. 'Darkside' coleus (*Solenostemon scutellarioides* 'Darkside', Zone 11)

3. 'Icicles' helichrysum (*Helichrysum thianschanicum* 'Icicles', Zones 10-11)

4. Variegated lantana (*Lantana camara* cv., Zone 11)

5. Napoleon™ papyrus (*Cyperus papyrus* Napoleon™, Zones 10-11)

6. 'Burgundy Wedding Train' coleus (*Solenostemon scutellarioides* 'Burgundy Wedding Train', Zone 11)

7. Variegated St. Augustine grass (*Stenotaphrum secundatus* 'Variegatum', Zones 9-11)

8. 'Frosted' geranium (*Pelargonium citrosum* 'Frosted', Zones 10-11)

9. Miscanthus (*Miscanthus sinensis* cv., Zones 4-9)

10. 'Sunset Velvet' oxalis (*Oxalis siliquosa* 'Sunset Velvet', Zones 8-10)

11. 'Tangletown's Dark Secret' coleus (*Solenostemon scutellarioides* 'Tangletown's Dark Secret', Zone 11)

White flowers add a sense of formality to a landscape. Here, they call attention to a home's entry and tie in with the home's painted trim. White-variegated foliage has a similar impact and also helps pull a planting together visually.

ABOVE Upright junipers lend themselves to trimming into twirling spires, adding an upright accent on either side of this front door. You can purchase these shrubs and trim them yourself or buy them already pruned from a nursery.

LEFT Mix and match an assortment of containers to create an informal entry for a cottage home. The eclectic nature of the pots and plantings serves as a conversation point when greeting guests on this front porch.

'Marmaduke' Rex begonia

'Vancouver Centennial' geranium

alternatives to coleus

 lthough coleus have become a mainstay in container gardening, there are alternatives with similar attributes if coleus just aren't your thing. Here are just a few.

LATIN NAME	COMMON NAME	KEY FEATURES
Pelargonium cvs.	Geraniums	Bright flowers and beautiful leaves—some variegated or scented
Begonia cvs.	Rex begonias	Broad range of bold, fascinating leaves and hairy stems
Hypoestes phyllostachya and cvs.	Polka-dot plants	Bright, variegated, and colorful foliage
Oxalis vulcanicola Zinfandel™	Oxalis	Burgundy, cloverlike foliage
Alternanthera ficoidea cvs.	Threadleaf alternanthera	Colorful, threadlike leaves

ABOVE Formal, symmetric architecture calls for formal containers and balanced, matching plantings. Here, that sense of symmetry is repeated both on the step piers and at the doorway.

RIGHT Containers are clustered on this front porch, flank the front steps, and are tucked into a front-yard border. The color scheme established in the garden is repeated in the container plantings.

Drama can be created even in the shade of a covered entry.
Assorted coleus, along with sweet potato vine, cordyline,
begonia, geranium, dracaena, calathea, and meadowsweet
show off their colorful foliage in this trio of pots.

Color-coordinating the container plantings on a front stoop with those in the garden can help tie a home to the surrounding landscape. The strong use of color also leads visitors to the front door.

The unlikely combination of moisture-loving Scotch moss and drought-tolerant agave in the foreground is achieved by planting a pot within a pot. This allows for different soil types and for the Scotch moss to be watered while the agave is kept dry. A pencil cactus provides some background drama.

a color combo to match the door

1. 'Wyoming' canna (*Canna* 'Wyoming', Zones 8-11)

2. 'Solar Flair' coleus (*Solenostemon scutellarioides* 'Solar Flair', Zone 11)

3. 'Gartenmeister Bonstedt' fuchsia (*Fuchsia* 'Gartenmeister Bonstedt', Zones 9-10)

4. Tropicanna® canna (*Canna indica* 'Phasion', Zones 8-11)

ferns and ivies thrive in a shady entry

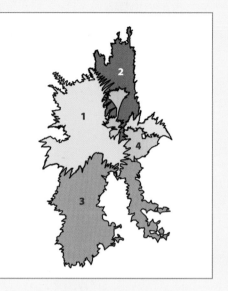

1. Autumn fern (*Dryopteris erythrosora*, Zones 6-9)

2. Upright plum yew (*Cephalotaxus harringtonia* 'Fastigiata', Zones 6-9)

3. Teardrop ivy (*Hedera helix* 'Teardrop', Zones 5-10)

4. Dwarf pieris (*Pieris japonica* 'Cavatine', Zones 6-8)

how shady is your site?

before buying plants, observe how much light and shade your site receives. Also keep in mind that the angle of the sun changes over the course of the gardening season and as trees leaf out, sun-and-shade patterns can be variable. While full sun means direct sun shines all day during the summer, there are several degrees of shade. Match the type of light on your site to the plant requirements noted on plant labels or in gardening reference books.

- **Light shade:** Plants get four to six hours of direct sun or a slight pattern of shade all day.

- **Partial shade:** Plants get two to four hours of sunlight or a pattern of dappled shade.

- **Full shade:** Plants receive only reflected, indirect light.

- **Dense shade:** There is little indirect light.

—Gary Keim

TOP The simplicity of this planting—a single geranium in a single, elegant, swan-shaped pot—helps create a calm setting for a small, shaded patio that marks the entry to a home's library.

LEFT An assortment of geraniums with bright flowers show off their different foliage patterns, dressing up the steps that lead from a cottage garden to a shady front porch.

• passageways

Steps are a natural spot for containers if for no other reason than the change in grade makes it easy to display them. Yet when placed on steps, they clearly announce a transition from one area to another. As long as there is clear passage, containers can actually enhance safety by calling attention to the grade change. Lining either side of a staircase is one approach, but staggering clusters on either side can encourage those passing through to slow down and enjoy the garden. Vines planted in containers can also be encouraged to scramble along railings or up and over a doorway or arbor. The same holds true along paths, where containers can highlight gates, arbors, and grade changes.

ABOVE Stone or brick piers often mark transitions between outdoor spaces and offer the perfect spot for a favorite container planting. Because they are raised above the rest of the garden and are closer to eye level, both the pot and plantings will undergo close inspection, so keep them looking fresh.

A small seating alcove was created along this gently curving backyard path. A bold, colorful New Zealand flax rises up from a weathered concrete container that displays a delightful been-there-forever look.

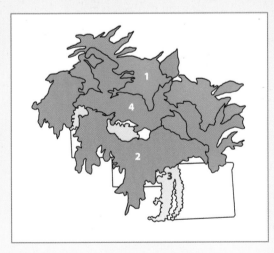

1. 'Gold Dust' croton (*Codiaeum variegatum* var. *pictum* 'Gold Dust', Zone 11)

2. 'Fusion Peach Frost' impatiens (*Impatiens* 'Fusion Peach Frost', annual)

3. Golden creeping Jenny (*Lysimachia nummularia* 'Aurea', Zones 4-8)

4. Bird's nest fern (*Asplenium nidus*, Zone 11)

color calls attention to grade change

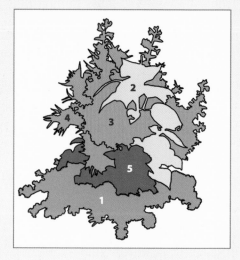

1. Razzle Dazzle® Cherry Dazzle® dwarf crape myrtle (*Lagerstroemia* 'Gamad I', Zones 6-9)

2. Copperleaf (*Acalypha wilkesiana* cv., Zones 10-11)

3. African mallow (*Anisodontea capensis*, Zones 8-9)

4. 'After Dark' Australian willow myrtle (*Agonis flexuosa* 'After Dark', Zones 10-11)

5. 'Grape Expectations' coleus (*Solenostemon scutellarioides* 'Grape Expectations', Zone 11)

ABOVE A vignette of ornaments and evergreen-filled containers stand out against a white fence, calling attention to the opening that provides passage between the side and backyards.

LEFT One of the simplest ways to use containers along steps is to set a series of matching pots and plants on each step. Impatiens are a good choice because of their long season of continuous bloom.

ABOVE This homeowner used containers of variegated hostas and ivies to signal grade changes. This is especially helpful when the treads of steps are made from the same materials as adjacent paths.

TOP RIGHT Matching pots with colorful glazes and burgundy-foliaged plants call attention to this narrow garden path that might otherwise be overlooked. Both the pots and plants are color coordinated with the garden.

RIGHT Container plantings can be used throughout a garden to direct traffic. In some cases, such as these steps, they lead you to a destination. In other cases, such as the pot at the edge of the narrowing path, they force you to slow down and inspect things more closely.

white variegation and flowers brighten a dark corner

1. King Tut® papyrus (*Cyperus papyrus* King Tut®, Zones 10-11)

2. Honey bush (*Melianthus major*, Zones 8-11)

3. Callie™ White calibrachoa (*Calibrachoa* Callie™ White, annual)

4. Variegated vinca (*Vinca major* 'Variegata', Zones 7-9)

gathering spaces

●●● TERRACES, DECKS, AND PORCHES undergo a major transformation when filled with containers. They bring the garden to your feet, soften hard surfaces, and make an empty space feel lush and inviting. They also help create the perfect atmosphere for an outdoor gathering, whether a romantic dinner for two or a garden party for dozens of your closest friends.

Think like a designer and not just a gardener—work the space. Start with containers flanking doorways and lining stairways. Cluster pots in corners and around posts or columns. Hang baskets from eaves, on walls, or from arbors. Line up a row of pots to create a living wall to break up large spaces and define more intimate gathering spaces. Cluster pots along a wall to create a focal point, perhaps tucking in a small fountain while you're at it. Use groupings of containers to frame or screen views.

Also think about color schemes and use repetition of form, texture, and color to tie the entire space together. Design an entire staged container garden along one or more walls to give the impression of a lush garden border.

ABOVE Containers are clustered in a vignette at a strategic point in this secret backyard getaway. There is also a planted trough atop a table that is created from an oversized ceramic pot topped with a cut-stone slab.

LEFT Big pots hold big plants. This large terra-cotta pot is host to several giant flowering tobacco plants and partially covered by trailing ivy. The terra-cotta blends in seamlessly with the brick paving and painted garden shed.

FACING PAGE A generous collection of planted containers softens the brick house and complements the natural stone patio, making it feel almost as if the chairs are set in the midst of an inground garden. The secret to achieving this look is packing the pots closely together and planting them with a variety of plant shapes and habits.

•patios and terraces

Patios and terraces are among the most popular places for containers. These spaces often serve as both destination and passageway to the extended landscape, so think about where the seating areas will be in relationship to passageways, and place your pots accordingly. When creating clusters, start with three pots—a large one that serves as a focal point and two smaller ones that serve a supporting role. Add additional pots as needed to fill the space. Obelisks and trellises can add an upright accent or create a sense of enclosure. If there are lots of pots, consider planting many with trees, shrubs, and perennials that will give the space a sense of maturity, reduce maintenance, and cut back on the number of plants you purchase from year to year.

ABOVE Bright blue pots draw your eyes across the lawn to this small destination patio. Once there, the fragrance of lilacs will make you want to linger just a little longer.

choosing a potting soil

container plants need soil that drains well yet holds some moisture and nutrients for plants. Most *garden soil* and *planting soil* is too heavy and dense for a container, and plants will languish in it. Instead, start with *potting soil* made specifically for container gardening. Many gardeners like to experiment and mix their own potting soils, but most store-bought potting soils with vermiculite or perlite and some kind of slow-release fertilizer will do just fine. If the store-bought kind is missing those ingredients, you can purchase them separately and mix them in sparingly.

Most potting soils also benefit from the generous addition (approximately one-third of the container) of compost; mushroom compost and rotted manure are good choices. If growing succulents or other xeric plants, mix in coarse sand or gravel to improve drainage. Keep in mind that the fertilizer included in the bag is just to get you started. You'll still need to add a slow-release fertilizer periodically or give plants a boost with liquid fertilizers every few weeks during the growing season.

LEFT This patio is surrounded by a mix of inground plantings and container plantings. The low, billowing and sprawling plants soften the space, camouflaging the bases of pots and edges of the paving.

RIGHT The matching pots of narrow, upright junipers make a striking contrast to the horizontal lines created from the stacked-stone wall, dining table, and row of paper lanterns on this small patio.

BELOW A lush garden setting is enhanced on this patio by using lots of foliage plants of different sizes placed at different heights surrounding the living spaces. Plants can be placed in pots of varying heights, as well as on steps, small tables, overturned pots, or bricks.

a dramatic patio vignette

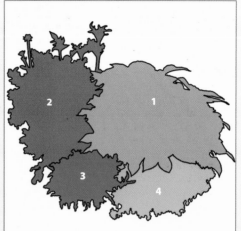

1. 'Spartacus' dahlia (*Dahlia* 'Spartacus', Zones 9-11)

2. 'Texas Parking Lot' coleus (*Solenostemon scutellarioides* 'Texas Parking Lot', Zone 11)

3. Million Bells® Terra Cotta calibrachoa (*Calibrachoa* Million Bells® Terra Cotta, annual)

4. 'Kiwi Fern' coleus (*Solenostemon scutellarioides* 'Kiwi Fern', Zone 11)

tinges of burgundy accent a southwest setting

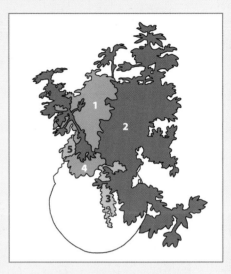

1. 'Rustic Orange' coleus (*Solenostemon scutellarioides* 'Rustic Orange', Zone 11)

2. 'Maple Sugar' hibiscus (*Hibiscus acetosella* 'Maple Sugar', Zones 10-11)

3. Golden creeping Jenny (*Lysimachia nummularia* 'Aurea', Zones 4-8)

4. 'Burgundy Glow' bugleweed (*Ajuga reptans* 'Burgundy Glow', Zones 3-9)

5. Golden variegated sage (*Salvia officinalis* 'Icterina', Zones 5-8)

TOP LEFT Containers can also be hung against walls. Here, a wire hayrack, or window basket, was attached to a wire trellis. This allows small vines to both scramble up the trellis and trail from the basket, covering a broad expanse of wall.

ABOVE If a terrace is surrounded by a retaining wall or raised seat wall, the wall can support lots of pots. Choose bold container plantings, like this one with petunias and silver plectranthus, to anchor the corners.

LEFT Another way to cover up a wall is to place trellises in large, rectangular pots or planters that rest on the ground. Here, vines climb up homemade copper trellises, covering the walls with flowers and foliage.

RIGHT Ferns and ivy spill from a deep-green ceramic pot placed along the edge of a hillside terrace. Pot feet ensure that excess moisture drains easily from the container.

FAR RIGHT Oversized Italian terra-cotta pots anchor the edge of a backyard terrace, helping to break up the long lines of paving. This strawberry jar, along with other pots, is planted with succulents, both a drought-tolerant choice and a nod to the Mediterranean-style home and containers.

A row of matching containers with small trees adds a vertical accent and visual interest to a broad, horizontal patio and an ivy-covered boundary wall. Variegated ivy flows from the pots to the paving.

Silver plectranthus

plants that perform well into fall

t ropical plants often steal the show in summer, but don't forget to create a backbone of sturdy plants that last from spring through fall—and potentially beyond. These plants are most memorable in fall.

LATIN NAME	COMMON NAME	KEY FEATURES
Cornus alba and *C. sericea*	Redtwig dogwood	Shrubs with spring flowers, colorful fall foliage, and red stems in winter
Heuchera spp. and cvs.	Coral bells	Beautifully shaped and colored foliage
Panicum virgatum 'Northwind'	'Northwind' switchgrass	Rigid, upright grass that doesn't flop in wind
Plectranthus spp. and cvs.	Plectranthus	Great foliage all season long; fall blooms
Pyracantha spp. and cvs.	Firethorn	Evergreen shrub with prolific fall berries
Osmanthus heterophyllus 'Goshiki'	'Goshiki' false holly	Stunning evergreen with pinkish leaves in spring that turn deep green
Sedum spp. and cvs.	Sedums	Wide range of succulents, colorful foliage

RIGHT This Victorian wire plant stand creates an old-fashioned atmosphere and is appropriately filled with old-fashioned plants like annual geraniums. The rabbit adds a playful accent.

BELOW Instead of a cut-flower arrangement, choose a container combination for your tabletop. Aromatic herbs are especially appropriate for a dining table, but other small flowering and foliage plants work equally well.

bold simplicity adds interest to a small gathering space

1. 'Anthole' begonia (*Begonia* 'Anthole', Zone 11)

2. Fiber-optic grass (*Isolepis cernua*, Zones 8-10)

3. Fiveleaf akebia (*Akebia quinata*, Zones 5-9)

• courtyards

Courtyards are unique in that there is typically ample wall space against which to place container plantings. Start with a single strong focal point and place plants around it. In an entry courtyard, this may be the front door. In other courtyards, it might be an area with sculpture or a fountain surrounded by lushly planted containers. Think about how the space should feel.

Calm spaces can be created by using lots of foliage in various shades of green and perhaps a few white or light-colored flowers. If a sense of energy is the goal, fill the space with tropicals or plants that produce lots of brightly colored flowers. A bubbling fountain made from an attractive container might also be a nice addition to the courtyard.

FACING PAGE Green ceramic pots are the perfect accent for this Mediterranean courtyard. Filled with drought-tolerant echeveria, senecio, and aeonium, they are ideally suited to hot, dry summers. The sheer volume of plants softens the hard surfaces of the walls and paving.

LEFT Containers are tucked all around this brick courtyard garden—on the terrace, anchoring the corners of the boxwood parterre, and as focal points in the parterres. They hold a mix of clipped boxwoods, evergreen standards, and flowering plants.

BELOW A half-dozen terra-cotta pots filled with papyrus create a watery allée in a Mediterranean-style courtyard. The repetition of a single strong planting and the geometric nature of both their placement and the canal give this garden a formal flair.

RIGHT Plants adorn an empty space, turning a tiny courtyard into a secret garden room. Containers are everywhere—on the ground, hanging along walls, and raised on supports. White flowers tie everything together visually.

BELOW A pair of bold matching planters with topiary shrubs add a touch of formality to this seating area.

EYE-CATCHING COMBINATIONS

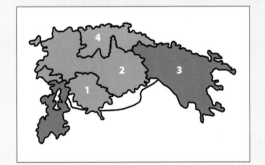

1. Golden Scotch moss (*Sagina subulata* 'Aurea', Zones 4-7)

2. 'Black Scallop' bugleweed (*Ajuga reptans* 'Black Scallop', Zones 3-9)

3. English ivy (*Hedera helix* cv., Zones 5-11)

4. Dark Dancer™ white clover (*Trifolium repens* 'Atropurpureum', Zones 4-10)

fine foliage separates large leaves

tiny, narrow, or fern-like foliage interspersed among large, dominant leaves is the glue that holds all the foliage together. Whether using the thriller-filler-spiller design technique, a planting-in-odd-numbers strategy, or focusing on color theory, your main focus should be using complementary textures. That will make it easy to create exciting container combinations—even if they're simply green.

—Rita Randolph

TOP LEFT Exuberant pots of hot-pink petunias anchor steps that lead from the house to a sunken courtyard garden filled with roses, boxwoods, and pink ivy geraniums. This space receives full sun in the summertime and suits the bold, bright colors.

LEFT This iron table and brick wall are adorned with assorted pots and hanging baskets filled with foliage plants. They are tucked among more sculptural accents to help create the look and feel of a comfortable outdoor room in a backyard courtyard.

FACING PAGE Nearly two-thirds of the floor space in this courtyard is devoted to plants, most of them in containers. This overhead view emphasizes the crucial role of foliage texture when creating plant combinations.

•decks and balconies

Decks and balconies, because they are raised above ground, greatly benefit from container gardens. This helps connect them to the broader landscape, as well as makes them feel cozy and protected. Containers can be arranged to preserve and frame desirable views while screening unwanted views. Window boxes hung from railings can be easily accessed for watering and routine care. Pots can be aligned or clustered to break up the expanse of a large deck to create a range of outdoor spaces—perhaps a dining area, a group seating space, or a cozy spot for two. Protect wooden decks from stains with pot feet that allow good drainage and air circulation, and consider using lighter-weight synthetic pots.

ABOVE Containers surround this deck, inside and out, creating a lush, green space for outdoor dining in warm, dry weather. They are filled primarily with hardy perennials, which return from year to year, even in pots.

RIGHT Succulents and a New Zealand flax fill a trio of containers that anchor the corner of a deck that is sunny for most of the day, but dips into shade when the sun ducks behind the house.

FACING PAGE Containers on an open deck can help connect the space to the surrounding landscape, frame views, and provide a sense of enclosure or intimacy. Ornamental grasses are especially nice on decks, as they sway with the wind without toppling the container.

RIGHT A cluster of tiny herbal topiaries sits atop this table on the corner of a ground-level deck. The larger container showcases the silvery foliage of cardoon and licorice plants.

BELOW The window basket hanging from this balcony railing can be enjoyed from indoors, while on the balcony, and from the yard. There is also a wall-mounted basket next to the door, close enough that it can be easily watered from the balcony.

intricate plants demand close inspection

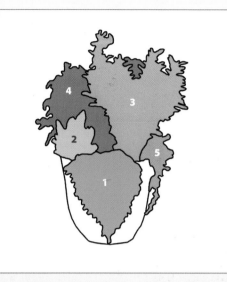

1. Variegated rupturewort (*Herniaria glabra* 'Sea Foam', Zones 5-8)

2. Paddle plant (*Kalanchoe thyrsiflora*, Zone 11)

3. Variegated pedilanthus (*Pedilanthus tithymaloides* 'Variegatus', Zones 10-11)

4. Fernleaf geranium (*Pelargonium denticulatum*, Zones 9-11)

5. Red-stemmed pilea (*Pilea* 'Red Stem', Zone 11)

RIGHT Matching balconies all decked out with matching and meticulously groomed topiaries dress up this townhouse. The tiered topiaries in the first-floor window boxes add a nice touch as well.

BELOW Plants create a sense of privacy on this deck, which sits on a narrow lot with views to neighboring backyards. Many of the plants were placed on benches to create a higher wall of greenery.

densely planted pots provide screening

1. Porcupine grass (*Miscanthus sinensis* 'Strictus', Zones 4-9)

2. Caribbean Sunset™ cuphea (*Cuphea cyanea* Caribbean Sunset™, Zones 9-11)

3. Foxtail fern (*Asparagus densiflorus* 'Meyersii', Zones 9-11)

4. Dinosaur kale (*Brassica oleracea* 'Nero di Toscana', annual)

5. Dream Kisses® Orange Sunset calibrachoa (*Calibrachoa* 'Wescaosa', annual)

6. Fernleaf geranium (*Pelargonium denticulatum*, Zones 9-11)

7. 'Indian Summer' black-eyed Susan (*Rudbeckia hirta* 'Indian Summer', Zones 3-7)

foliage plants dress up a shady deck

1. 'Prince of Orange' philodendron (*Philodendron* 'Prince of Orange', Zone 11)

2. 'Laurentii' snake plant (*Sansevieria trifasciata* 'Laurentii', Zone 11)

3. 'Macho' fern (*Nephrolepis biserrata* 'Macho', Zones 9-11)

4. 'Forever Midi Orange Glow' kalanchoe (*Kalanchoe* 'Forever Midi Orange Glow', Zone 11)

5. 'Troy's Gold' plectranthus (*Plectranthus ciliatus* 'Troy's Gold', Zones 10-11)

ABOVE Plants help make a big space feel more intimate. Clusters of plantings on this deck are created around bold foliage plants such as the Abyssinian banana, with big, reddish leaves, and the New Zealand flax with strappy, burgundy leaves.

LEFT Containers can be arranged around deck chairs as if they were end tables or stacks of books. They work almost like fabric in an indoor room, adding color, texture, and a soft touch to a space.

• rooftops

What could be better than viewing a sunrise or sunset over the city from your own private garden? Rooftop container gardens are a great way to add green space to urban landscapes. Special considerations do apply to rooftop gardens, though, so be sure to check with property owners or local authorities regarding any weight limits or other restrictions. Choose lightweight pots made from plastic and synthetic materials, when possible, and ensure that any trees and shrubs are securely anchored so they don't blow over in a storm. For this reason, pots should also be kept away from ledges. Make sure you have access to water and drainage systems, and think through your route and process for moving both fresh and spent plants, as well as other materials, through your building.

ABOVE A collection of drought-tolerant succulents and other xeric plants thrive in troughs and pots on a sunny rooftop. They need minimal care and can handle the often brutal heat.

RIGHT These carefully tended and trained herbal topiaries don't take up much space, so they can be tucked into narrow balcony and rooftop spaces where they can bask in the blazing sun.

ABOVE These concrete cylinders aren't likely to blow over in a storm. They look a bit like miniature buildings against this southern cityscape, where they sit on a green roof planted with succulents.

LEFT Between the twig structure and container plantings, you would think you were hanging out in a treehouse rather than on a New York City rooftop. Even vines and small trees can be grown on a rooftop if they are adequately anchored.

•poolside

Containers are right at home around a pool deck, where they can add a splash of color, anchor a seating area, or help screen views. Bold tropical plants such as palms, bananas, and cannas look especially at home around a pool and benefit from the full sun, but other types of plants and styles of planting are equally appropriate and can help tie the pool to your home's architecture and the surrounding landscape. Place containers on tabletops, cluster them in corners, position them on either side of entry gates and passageways, hang them from the windows of pool houses, and use them to break up the space along fences. Since most pools are located in full sun, choosing oversized pots rather than small pots will reduce watering needs.

The stone-colored and rough-surfaced pot, along with its blue-green succulents, blends right into the blue-green interior of the pool it's placed near.

ABOVE Pool decks are often large expanses of concrete or other paving, so they benefit from clusters of eye-catching containers. The containers visually break up the space, adding form, texture, height, and color.

FACING PAGE Don't underestimate the power of a single large pot. This one stands out as a focal point in the poolscape and is in keeping with the neat, clean look of the pool, lawn, and far border.

Heated pools can be enjoyed well into the fall, when tropical plantings may be past their peak. This is the perfect time for a fall container filled with red fountain grass or other fall favorites.

This cluster of colorful pots was assembled on a pool deck. Because they are large, they don't have to be watered as often. Using large pots around pools, which are frequently located in full sun and at some distance from the water spigot, is a good strategy.

a heat-tolerant combo

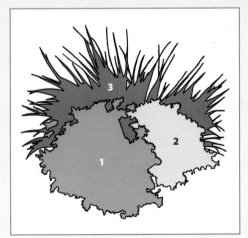

1. Lemon Symphony African daisy (*Osteospermum* 'Seikilrem', Zones 9-11)

2. 'Sunny Serena' African daisy (*Osteospermum* 'Sunny Serena', Zones 9-11)

3. Butterfly iris (*Dietes grandiflora*, Zones 9-11)

gardens

●●● CONTAINERS HAVE PLAYED AN IMPORTANT role in gardens for centuries, especially in formal gardens, where they are often used to reinforce the geometry of beds and borders. They can anchor the corners or play a starring role in the center of a formal bed or parterre. Likewise, they may serve as the focal point at the end of a path or be placed along either side of a passageway to create a sense of rhythm. Most formal gardens have a strong sense of balance, so it is natural for container plantings to follow this cue with symmetric, clipped, and matched plantings.

Containers are equally at home in informal gardens, regardless of style. Even naturalistic gardens filled with gently waving grasses, loose shrubs, and sprawling perennials benefit from the addition of a well-chosen container. With or without plants, containers are a welcome addition to borders, where they can double as sculptural focal points. Container plantings can also be used to fill temporary gaps in borders or to tuck in spots of color.

This stately pot was placed on an axis in the garden to draw your eye down the garden path from the pergola. Two equally large planted pots flank either side of the pathway.

This pot of bright red annuals was placed in a border where a shot of color was needed. As the season progresses, other pots can be placed in this spot, or something more permanent can be planted in the garden.

ABOVE A group of three pots provides a visual anchor for this rose-covered arbor post, making a strong connection with the surrounding garden. Clustering pots in odd-numbered groupings almost always creates a pleasing arrangement.

LEFT Pots can be raised up above a garden as well as tucked in among the plantings. In this case, both the painted pot and flowers echo the colors in the surrounding garden.

•beds and borders

Regardless of the style garden, containers can play both starring and supporting roles in beds and borders. Place pots in borders at ground level or raised on pedestals. Set them atop stone walls and pillars, anchoring gateways and arbors, or along a garden path. Think about using them strategically to draw the eye through a space, to add height to low plantings, or to frame views. If the pot itself is the main attraction, limit the trailing plants and set it apart from inground plantings. If the pot is simply a container, it can be more easily tucked in anywhere and filled with overflowing plants.

ABOVE The pink flowers and light, variegated foliage of 'Firecracker' fuchsia brighten a shady border. The lacy fern foliage and blue bugleweed flowers make for interesting textural and color contrasts.

RIGHT A large container of bright yarrow provides a bright spot of color in a free-spirited cottage garden. Lamb's ears and santolina engulf the base of the container, visually integrating it into the garden. A small citrus tree in the pot adds height.

box planter anchors a patio corner

1. Coleus (*Solenostemon scutellarioides* cv., Zone 11)

2. Nonstop® Yellow tuberous begonia (*Begonia* Nonstop Yellow, Zones 9-11)

3. 'Limelight' licorice plant (*Helichrysum petiolare* 'Limelight', Zones 10-11)

big pot with big foliage holds down a street-side border

1. 'Crystal White' zinnia (*Zinnia angustifolia* 'Crystal White', annual)

2. 'Crystal Palace Gem' geranium (*Pelargonium* 'Crystal Palace Gem', annual)

3. 'Illustris' elephant's ear (*Colocasia esculenta* 'Illustris', Zones 8-11)

fill the pot to the brim with plants that have similar needs

Visitors to my greenhouse often ask how many plants they can safely put in a pot. Plants grow until they touch and mingle anyway, so really filling a pot is quite acceptable. Just make sure that all the plants have compatible growing habits and that one eager grower won't take over the others. You can usually find all of this information on the plant tag, but ask questions at the nursery if you've picked a plant that doesn't include growing requirements.

—*Rita Randolph*

You can pack more plants per square inch in a pot than in the ground because their roots are contained and they can quickly find the nourishment they need. In the ground, plants tend to ramble, uncontrolled, looking for space to send their roots and spread their foliage.

Container plantings make the garden larger, extending plantings beyond garden beds. They also provide an excellent place for trying out new plants before giving them a more permanent home in a bed or border.

LEFT This classic container is tucked deep into a mixed border of trees, shrubs, and perennials. The white flowers and light pot stand out among the greenery.

BELOW The smooth surface of this container provides a contrasting backdrop for the grassy plants in the foreground, while the flowers provide a soft yet eye-catching color contrast in this shady border.

soothing colors blend into a border

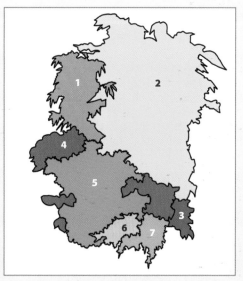

1. 'Maple Sugar' hibiscus (*Hibiscus acetosella* 'Maple Sugar', Zones 9-11)

2. Flowering maple (*Abutilon* cv., Zones 8-11)

3. 'Pink Chaos' coleus (*Solenostemon scutellarioides* 'Pink Chaos', Zone 11)

4. 'Trailing Queen' coleus (*Solenostemon scutellarioides* 'Trailing Queen', Zone 11)

5. Geranium (*Pelargonium* cv., Zone 11)

6. Diamond Frost® euphorbia (*Euphorbia* 'Inneuphdia', Zones 10-11)

7. Shadow Dancer® Violette fuchsia (*Fuchsia* 'Goetzviol', Zones 9-11)

•garden focal points

To make a container a focal point in the garden, start with a really great-looking container, one that is bigger than you might normally choose so that it stands out among plantings and other garden accents. Place it centrally, at the end of a long pathway or line of sight, or higher than surrounding elements. And then fill it with eye-catching plants—whether a single, architecturally striking plant or a bold combination of plants. Keep in mind that white and red flowers and foliage will better grab attention, while shades of blue, purple, and green will tend to recede in view. Formal plantings, such as topiaries or clipped boxwoods, are also excellent choices for containers serving as focal points.

ABOVE A pot of agapanthus serves as a focal point in the garden for several reasons: The pot is raised on a post; the light-colored post and pot stand out against the darker evergreen foliage; and the agapanthus flowers provide a spot of color.

RIGHT A short post and tall planter raise this container to new heights, showcasing a successful combination of thrillers, fillers, and spillers including purple fountain grass, 'Bellingrath Pink' coleus, and 'Margarita' sweet potato vine.

Blue is a unique color for the garden that always draws attention. So does a large pot with bold foliage placed centrally or along an axis. This one wins on both counts and serves as a destination in the garden.

a pot perks up a quiet spot in the garden

1. Spineless prickly pear cactus (*Opuntia ellisiana*, Zones 7-10)

2. Golden creeping Jenny (*Lysimachia nummularia* 'Aurea', Zones 4-8)

3. Jovibarba (*Jovibarba hirta*, Zones 10-11)

4. 'Chocolate Soldier' panda plant (*Kalanchoe tomentosa* 'Chocolate Soldier', Zones 10-11)

ABOVE Old wagons and wheelbarrows can be filled with colorful container plantings and moved about the garden as needed for a change of scenery. They especially stand out against a smooth swath of lawn.

LEFT The use of putti statuary and white flowers hails from classic garden design practices. This deep, shady border benefits from the structure introduced by the putti planter, which helps break up the fine foliage textures.

ABOVE A Chinese juniper in a large container serves as a bold focal point at the end of an olive allée. It stands out because it is oversized, backlit, and aligned with the path.

TOP RIGHT A variegated century plant and sedum fill a shallow iron planter that is raised atop a stone pedestal. The broad, smooth, and upright leaves of the century plant provide a striking contrast to the finely textured foliage in the garden.

RIGHT This bright combination was planted in a hanging basket rather than a pot to achieve fullness. It is filled with cordyline, Dragon Wing® begonia, licorice plant, and 'Sweet Caroline Purple' sweet potato vine.

front-yard focal point for an historic neighborhood

1. 'Black Magic' elephant's ear (*Colocasia esculenta* 'Black Magic', Zones 8-11)

2. Octopus agave (*Agave vilmoriniana*, Zones 9-11)

3. 'Red Trailing Queen' coleus (*Solenostemon scutellarioides* 'Red Trailing Queen', Zone 11)

4. Nasturtium (*Tropaeolum majus* cv., annual)

5. Black-eyed Susan vine (*Thunbergia alata,* annual)

6. 'King's Gold' false cypress (*Chamaecyparis pisifera* 'King's Gold', Zones 4-8)

usda hardiness zone map

The zones stated in this book are based on several sources and should be treated as general guidelines when selecting plants for your garden. Many other factors may come into play in determining healthy plant growth. Microclimates, wind, soil type, soil moisture, humidity, snow, and winter sunshine may greatly affect the adaptability of plants. For more information and to zoom in on your area, visit the map online at www.usna.usda.gov/Hardzone/ushzmap.html.

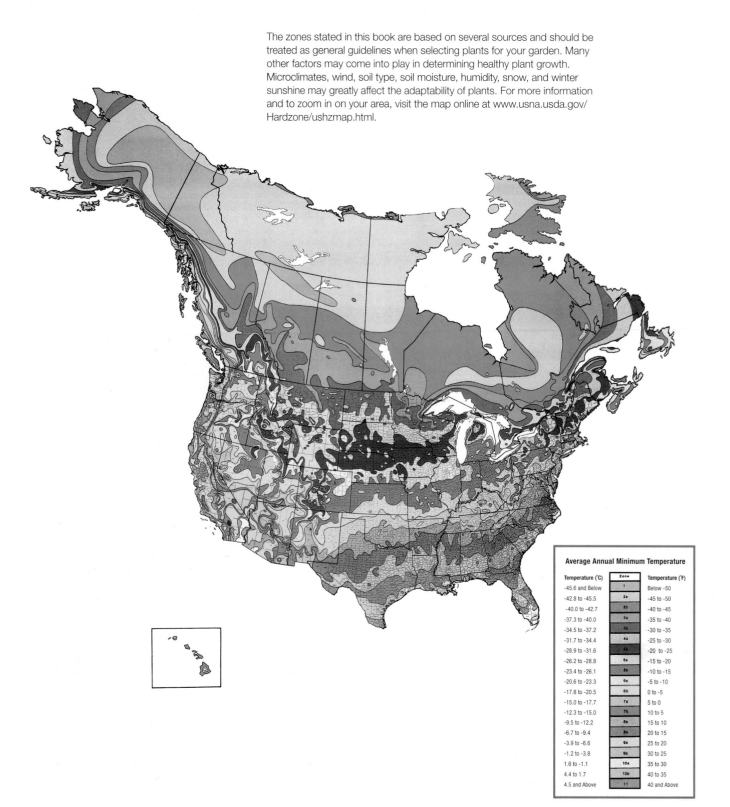

Average Annual Minimum Temperature		
Temperature (°C)	**Zone**	**Temperature (°F)**
-45.6 and Below	1	Below -50
-42.8 to -45.5	2a	-45 to -50
-40.0 to -42.7	2b	-40 to -45
-37.3 to -40.0	3a	-35 to -40
-34.5 to -37.2	3b	-30 to -35
-31.7 to -34.4	4a	-25 to -30
-28.9 to -31.6	4b	-20 to -25
-26.2 to -28.8	5a	-15 to -20
-23.4 to -26.1	5b	-10 to -15
-20.6 to -23.3	6a	-5 to -10
-17.8 to -20.5	6b	0 to -5
-15.0 to -17.7	7a	5 to 0
-12.3 to -15.0	7b	10 to 5
-9.5 to -12.2	8a	15 to 10
-6.7 to -9.4	8b	20 to 15
-3.9 to -6.6	9a	25 to 20
-1.2 to -3.8	9b	30 to 25
1.6 to -1.1	10a	35 to 30
4.4 to 1.7	10b	40 to 35
4.5 and Above	11	40 and Above

photo credits

p. ii–iii: Jennifer Benner, courtesy Fine Gardening magazine, © The Taunton Press, Inc.

p. v: Brandi Spade, courtesy Fine Gardening magazine, © The Taunton Press, Inc. (top left); Deanne Fortnam (top right); Michelle Gervais, courtesy Fine Gardening magazine, © The Taunton Press, Inc. (bottom left); Rizanino Reyes (bottom right)

p. vi: Brandi Spade, courtesy Fine Gardening magazine, © The Taunton Press, Inc.

CHAPTER 1

p. 4: © Lee Anne White

p 6 © Lee Anne White (left); © Steve Silk; design: Loomis Creek Nursery (right)

p. 7: Brandi Spade, courtesy Fine Gardening magazine, © The Taunton Press, Inc.

p. 8: © Lee Anne White (top); Jennifer Benner, courtesy Fine Gardening magazine, © The Taunton Press; design: Ilene Sternberg (bottom)

p. 9: Courtesy Jill Goodsell; design: Jill Goodsell (left); Fine Gardening staff, © The Taunton Press, Inc. (right)

p. 10: © Lee Anne White

p. 11: © Lee Anne White; design: David McMullin (left); Jennifer Benner, courtesy Fine Gardening magazine, © The Taunton Press, Inc. (right)

p. 12: © Lee Anne White (top and bottom)

p. 13: Brandi Spade, courtesy Fine Gardening magazine, © The Taunton Press, Inc.

p. 14: © Lee Anne White (left); © Mick Hales (right)

p. 15: Brandi Spade, courtesy Fine Gardening magazine, © The Taunton Press, Inc.

p. 16: © Lee Anne White (top); © Lee Anne White; design: Loise Poer (bottom)

p. 17: Brandi Spade, courtesy Fine Gardening magazine, © The Taunton Press, Inc.

p. 18: © Mick Hales (left); © Lee Anne White (right)

p. 19: Brandi Spade, courtesy Fine Gardening magazine, © The Taunton Press, Inc.

p. 20: © Lee Anne White

p. 21: © Lee Anne White (top); © Lee Anne White; design: Ryan Gainey (bottom)

p. 22: Holly Lepere Photography, © Grace Design Associates (left); © Lee Anne White; design: Keeyla Meadows (right)

p. 23: Michelle Gervais, courtesy Fine Gardening magazine, © The Taunton Press, Inc.; design: Rebecca Sweet (top); © Lee Anne White; design: Michelle Derviss (bottom)

p. 24: © Lee Anne White; Carolyn & Gary Palmer garden (top); © Lee Anne White; design: Groupworks (bottom left); © Mick Hales

p. 25: Virginia Small, courtesy Fine Gardening magazine, © The Taunton Press, Inc.

p. 26: © Lee Anne White; design: Saul Nursery (left); Todd Meier, courtesy Fine Gardening magazine, © The Taunton Press, Inc.; design: Nancy Goodwin (right)

p. 27: Brandi Spade, courtesy Fine Gardening magazine, © The Taunton Press, Inc.

p. 28: Jennifer Benner, courtesy Fine Gardening magazine, © The Taunton Press, Inc.; design: Julia Janiak

p. 29: © Lee Anne White; design: Jon Carloftis (left); © Lee Anne White

p. 30: © Lee Anne White (top and bottom)

p. 31: © Lee Anne White; design: Jennifer Romberg

p. 32: © Lee Anne White (left); © Lee Anne White; design: DaVida Pools (right)

p. 33: Melissa Lucas

p. 34: Michelle Gervais, courtesy Fine Gardening magazine, © The Taunton Press, Inc. (top); © Lee Anne White; design: Michelle Derviss (bottom)

p. 35: Brandi Spade, courtesy Fine Gardening magazine, © The Taunton Press, Inc.

p. 36: Holly Lepere Photography, © Grace Design Associates

p. 37: © Lee Anne White; design: Frances Dixon (top); Michelle Gervais, courtesy Fine Gardening magazine, © The Taunton Press, Inc. (bottom)

p. 38: © Lee Anne White (all)

p. 39: Michelle Gervais, courtesy Fine Gardening magazine, © The Taunton Press, Inc.

CHAPTER 2

p. 40: © Steve Silk, design: Sydney Eddison

p. 42: © Lee Anne White; design: Saul Nursery (left); © Mick Hales (right)

p. 43: Deanne Fortnam

p. 44: Kat White

p. 45: Michelle Gervais, courtesy Fine Gardening magazine, © The Taunton Press, Inc. (top); © Steve Silk (bottom left); © Lee Anne White; design: The Fockele Garden Company (bottom right)

p. 46: © Lee Anne White (left); © Mick Hales (right)

p. 47: Michelle Gervais, courtesy Fine Gardening magazine, © The Taunton Press, Inc.

p. 48: © Lee Anne White; design: Saul Nursery (left); Fine Gardening staff, © The Taunton Press, Inc. (right)

p. 49: Jennifer Benner, courtesy Fine Gardening magazine, © The Taunton Press, Inc.

p. 50: Colleen Fitzpatrick

p. 51: Scott Endres (top); courtesy Fine Gardening magazine, © The Taunton Press, Inc,; design: Gary Keim (bottom)

p. 52: © Lee Anne White; design: Saul Nursery (left); © Steve Silk (right)

p. 53: © Lee Anne White; design: Saul Nursery

p. 54: Michelle Gervais, courtesy Fine Gardening magazine, © The Taunton Press, Inc.

p. 55: © Mick Hales (left); Danielle Sherry, courtesy Fine Gardening magazine, © The Taunton Press, Inc. (right)

p. 56: Heather Geiser; design: Heather Geiser (top left); © Mick Hales (bottom left); Jennifer Benner, courtesy Fine Gardening magazine, © The Taunton Press, Inc. (right)

p. 57: Rizanini Reyes

p. 58: © Mick Hales

p. 59: Michelle Gervais, courtesy Fine Gardening magazine, © The Taunton Press, Inc.

p. 60: Todd Holloway; © Lee Anne White; design: Keeyla Meadows (right)

p. 61: Rita Randolph

p. 62: Michelle Gervais, courtesy Fine Gardening magazine, © The Taunton Press, Inc.

p. 63: © Lee Anne White; design: Keeyla Meadows (left); Danielle Sherry, courtesy Fine Gardening magazine, © The Taunton Press, Inc.; design: Barbara Weirich (right)

p. 64: Michelle Gervais, courtesy Fine Gardening magazine, © The Taunton Press, Inc.

p. 65: Jimmy Turner (top); © Lee Anne White (bottom)

p. 66: Michelle Gervais, courtesy Fine Gardening magazine, © The Taunton Press, Inc. (top); © Lee Anne White; design: Saul Nursery (bottom)

p. 67: Michelle Gervais, courtesy Fine Gardening magazine, © The Taunton Press, Inc.

p. 68: Scott Endres

p. 69: Michelle Gervais, courtesy Fine Gardening magazine, © The Taunton Press, Inc. (left); courtesy Fine Gardening magazine, © The Taunton Press, Inc.; design: Cynthia Fletcher

p. 70:courtesy Fine Gardening magazine, © The Taunton Press, Inc.;<it> design: Cynthia Fletcher

p. 71: Brandi Spade, courtesy Fine Gardening magazine, © The Taunton Press, Inc.; design: Carter Lee Clapsadle (top); © Lee Anne White (bottom)

p. 72: © Lee Anne White; design: Sydney Eddison

p. 73: © Lee Anne White (top); courtesy Fine Gardening magazine, © The Taunton Press, Inc.; design: Cynthia Fletcher

p. 74: © Lee Anne White; design: Jeni Webber (top); © Steve Silk (bottom)

p. 75: Brandi Spade, courtesy Fine Gardening

magazine, © The Taunton Press, Inc.

p. 76: © Steve Silk

p. 77: © Steve Silk (top); © Steve Silk; design: Loomis Creek Nursery (bottom)

p. 78: © Mick Hales

p. 79: Deanne Fortnam

p. 80: Fine Gardening staff, © The Taunton Press, Inc. (top and bottom)

p. 81: Michelle Gervais, courtesy Fine Gardening magazine, © The Taunton Press, Inc. (top); © Lee Anne White; design: David Feix (bottom)

p. 82: Michelle Gervais, courtesy Fine Gardening magazine, © The Taunton Press, Inc.

p. 83: Leslie Schaler (top); Jacqueline Kock; design: Barbara Libner (bottom)

p. 84: Michelle Gervais, courtesy Fine Gardening magazine, © The Taunton Press, Inc.

p. 85: Fine Gardening staff, © The Taunton Press, Inc.

p. 86: Michelle Gervais, courtesy Fine Gardening magazine, © The Taunton Press, Inc. (top); Steve Aitken, courtesy Fine Gardening magazine, © The Taunton Press, Inc. (bottom)

p. 87: Fine Gardening staff, © The Taunton Press, Inc.

p. 88: Michelle Gervais, courtesy Fine Gardening magazine, © The Taunton Press, Inc. (top left and top right); Jennifer Benner, courtesy Fine Gardening magazine, © The Taunton Press, Inc. (top center); © Lee Anne White; design: Saul Nursery (bottom)

p. 89: Melissa Lucas; design Longwood Gardens

p. 90: © Lee Anne White; design: Ben Page, Jr. (top); Jennifer Benner, courtesy Fine Gardening magazine, © The Taunton Press, Inc.; (bottom)

p. 91: Michelle Gervais, courtesy Fine Gardening magazine, © The Taunton Press, Inc.

CHAPTER 3

p. 92: Holly Lepere Photography, © Grace Design Associates

p. 94: Holly Lepere Photography, © Grace Design Associates (left and right)

p. 95: Michelle Gervais, courtesy Fine Gardening magazine, © The Taunton Press, Inc.

p. 96: © Lee Anne White; design: Saul Nursery (top); © Lee Anne White

p. 97: Michelle Gervais, courtesy Fine Gardening magazine, © The Taunton Press, Inc.

p. 98: © Lee Anne White

p. 99: © Lee Anne White (left); Holly Lepere Photography, © Grace Design Associates (right)

p. 100: Holly Lepere Photography, © Grace Design Associates (left); © Lee Anne White

p. 101: Michelle Gervais, courtesy Fine Gardening magazine, © The Taunton Press,

Inc.

p. 102: © Lee Anne White

p. 103: © Lee Anne White; design: Scott Melcher (top); © Lee Anne White; design: Louise Poer (bottom)

p. 104: © Lee Anne White; design: Saul Nursery

p. 105: © Lee Anne White; design: Dan Cleveland (top); © Lee Anne White; design: Anne Sheldon

p. 106: © Mick Hales; design: Shakespeare's Garden

p. 107: © Mick Hales (left and right)

p. 108: © Lee Anne White; design: Ann Sheldon (left); © Lee Anne White; design: Saul Nursery (right)

p. 109: © Lee Anne White; design: Robin & Paul Cowley

p. 110: © Steve Silk (top); © Lee Anne White; design: Ryan Gainey (bottom)

p. 111: © Lee Anne White

p. 112: Jennifer Benner, courtesy Fine Gardening magazine, © The Taunton Press, Inc. (left); Michelle Gervais, courtesy Fine Gardening magazine, © The Taunton Press, Inc. (right)

p. 113: © Steve Silk

p. 114: © Saxon Holt (left); © Lee Anne White; design: Ann Sheldon

p. 115: Holly Lepere Photography, © Grace Design Associates

p. 116: Steve Aitken, courtesy Fine Gardening magazine, © The Taunton Press, Inc. (top left); Michelle Gervais, courtesy Fine Gardening magazine, © The Taunton Press, Inc. (top right); © Saxon Holt; design: Frederique Lavoipierre (bottom left); Scott Phillips, courtesy Fine Gardening magazine, © The Taunton Press, Inc. (bottom right)

p. 117: © Saxon Holt; design: Frederique Lavoipierre

p. 118: © Lee Anne White (left and right)

p. 119: Jennifer Benner, courtesy Fine Gardening magazine, © The Taunton Press, Inc. (left and right)

p. 120: Danielle Sherry, courtesy Fine Gardening magazine, © The Taunton Press, Inc. (top); Brandi Spade, courtesy Fine Gardening magazine, © The Taunton Press, Inc. (bottom)

p. 121: © Lee Anne White

p. 122: Brandi Spade, courtesy Fine Gardening magazine, © The Taunton Press, Inc.;design: Julia Hofley (left); Brandi Spade, courtesy Fine Gardening magazine, © The Taunton Press, Inc. (right)

p. 123: Brandi Spade, courtesy Fine Gardening magazine, © The Taunton Press, Inc.

p. 124: © Mick Hales (left and right)

p. 125: © Lee Anne White; design: Saul Nursery

p. 126: © Mick Hales (top); Michelle Gervais, courtesy Fine Gardening magazine, © The Taunton Press, Inc.

p. 127: Michelle Gervais, courtesy Fine

Gardening magazine, © The Taunton Press, Inc.

p. 128: Michelle Gervais, courtesy Fine Gardening magazine, © The Taunton Press, Inc. (top); © Lee Anne White

p. 129: Michelle Gervais, courtesy Fine Gardening magazine, © The Taunton Press, Inc.

p. 130: © Lee Anne White

p. 131: Michelle Gervais, courtesy Fine Gardening magazine, © The Taunton Press, Inc.

p. 132: Michelle Gervais, courtesy Fine Gardening magazine, © The Taunton Press, Inc.

p. 133: © Lee Anne White; design: DaVida Pools

p. 134: © Lee Anne White; design: Saul Nursery (left); Jennifer Benner, courtesy Fine Gardening magazine, © The Taunton Press, Inc.; design: Robert Scanzavoli, Longwood Gardens (right)

p. 135: Michelle Gervais, courtesy Fine Gardening magazine, © The Taunton Press, Inc.

p. 136: © Mick Hales (left and right)

p. 137: Michelle Gervais, courtesy Fine Gardening magazine, © The Taunton Press, Inc.

p. 138: Michelle Gervais, courtesy Fine Gardening magazine, © The Taunton Press, Inc.

p. 139: © Mick Hales (left); Michelle Gervais, courtesy Fine Gardening magazine, © The Taunton Press, Inc.

p. 140: © Lee Anne White (left); © Mick Hales

141: Michelle Gervais, courtesy Fine Gardening magazine, © The Taunton Press, Inc.

CHAPTER 4

p. 142: Holly Lepere Photography, © Grace Design Associates

p. 144: © Lee Anne White (top left); Michelle Gervais, courtesy Fine Gardening magazine, © The Taunton Press, Inc. (bottom left); © Mick Hales (right)

p. 145: Kerry Ann Moore, courtesy Fine Gardening magazine, © The Taunton Press, Inc.

p. 146: © Mick Hales

p. 147: © Mick Hales (left); © Lee Anne White

p. 148: Holly Lepere Photography, © Grace Design Associates (top); Danielle Sherry, courtesy Fine Gardening magazine, © The Taunton Press, Inc. (bottom left and bottom right)

p. 149: Brandi Spade, courtesy Fine Gardening magazine, © The Taunton Press, Inc.

p. 150: Brandi Spade, courtesy Fine Gardening magazine, © The Taunton Press, Inc.

p. 151: Michelle Gervais, courtesy Fine Gardening magazine, © The Taunton Press, Inc. (top left); © Mick Hales (bottom left); Danielle Sherry, courtesy Fine Gardening magazine, © The Taunton Press, Inc.

p. 152: Brandi Spade, courtesy Fine Gardening magazine, © The Taunton Press, Inc.

p. 153: © Mick Hales (top); © Lee Anne White (bottom left and bottom right)

p. 154: Michelle Gervais, courtesy Fine Gardening magazine, © The Taunton Press, Inc. (top left); Brandi Spade, courtesy Fine Gardening magazine, © The Taunton Press, Inc. (top right); © Lee Anne White (bottom left); Danielle Sherry, courtesy Fine Gardening magazine, © The Taunton Press, Inc.

p. 155: Darryl Beyers, courtesy Fine Gardening magazine, © The Taunton Press, Inc.

p. 156: © Lee Anne White (left); Brandi Spade, courtesy Fine Gardening magazine, © The Taunton Press, Inc. (right)

p. 157: Brandi Spade, courtesy Fine Gardening magazine, © The Taunton Press, Inc.

p. 158: © Lee Anne White; design: The Fockele Garden Company

p. 159: © Lee Anne White (top and bottom)

p. 160: © Lee Anne White; design: David Thorne Landscape Architects (left); Michelle Gervais, courtesy Fine Gardening magazine, © The Taunton Press, Inc. (right)

p. 161: Brandi Spade, courtesy Fine Gardening magazine, © The Taunton Press, Inc.

p. 162: Michelle Gervais, courtesy Fine Gardening magazine, © The Taunton Press, Inc.

p. 163: © Lee Anne White; design: Dan Cleveland (top); Jennifer Benner, courtesy Fine Gardening magazine, © The Taunton Press, Inc. (bottom)

164: © Mick Hales (top left); © Steve Silk (top right); Lucy Hardiman (bottom)

p. 165: Brandi Spade, courtesy Fine Gardening magazine, © The Taunton Press, Inc.

p. 166: © Steve Silk

p. 167: © Lee Anne White (left); Virginia Small, courtesy Fine Gardening magazine, © The Taunton Press, Inc. (right)

p. 168: © Steve Silk

p. 168-169: Danielle Sherry, courtesy Fine Gardening magazine, © The Taunton Press, Inc.

p. 169 Krista Hick Benson, courtesy Fine Gardening magazine, © The Taunton Press, Inc. (top right)

p. 170: © Lee Anne White; design: Ryan Gainey (top); Brandi Spade, courtesy Fine Gardening magazine, © The Taunton Press, Inc.; design: Darcy Daniels (bottom)

p. 171: Michelle Gervais, courtesy Fine Gardening magazine, © The Taunton Press, Inc.

p. 172: Jesse Winters; design: Theresa Prebish & Jamie Schmitt

p. 173: Lucy Hardiman (top left and bottom left); Fine Gardening staff, © The Taunton Press, Inc. (right)

p. 174: © Lee Anne White; design: The Fockele Garden Company (top left); © Lee Anne White; design: David McMullin (top right); © Mick Hales (bottom)

p. 175: Michelle Gervais, courtesy Fine

Gardening magazine, © The Taunton Press, Inc.

p. 176: © Lee Anne White (top); Stephanie Fagan, courtesy Fine Gardening magazine, © The Taunton Press, Inc.

p. 177: Brandi Spade, courtesy Fine Gardening magazine, © The Taunton Press, Inc.

p. 178: Holly Lepere Photography, © Grace Design Associates

p. 179: © Lee Anne White; design: Louise Poer (top); © Steve Silk; design: Chanticleer Gardens (bottom)

p. 180: Lucy Hardiman (top); © Mick Hales (bottom)

p. 181: Brandi Spade, courtesy Fine Gardening magazine, © The Taunton Press, Inc.

p. 182: Fine Gardening staff, © The Taunton Press, Inc.

p. 183: Holly Lepere Photography, © Grace Design Associates (top left); courtesy Rita Randolph (top right); © Lee Anne White; design: Louise Poer (bottom)

p. 184: © Lee Anne White (left and right)

p. 185: © Lee Anne White

p. 186: © Lee Anne White (top and bottom)

p. 187: Brandi Spade, courtesy Fine Gardening magazine, © The Taunton Press, Inc.

p. 188: © Mick Hales (top); © Lee Anne White (bottom)

p. 189: Brandi Spade, courtesy Fine Gardening magazine, © The Taunton Press, Inc.

p. 190: Michelle Gervais, courtesy Fine Gardening magazine, © The Taunton Press, Inc.

p. 191: © Lee Anne White; design: Lee Anne White (top and bottom)

p. 192: © Mick Hales (left and right)

p. 193: © Mick Hales (left); © Lee Anne White

p. 194: © Lee Anne White; design: Bobby Saul (top); © Lee Anne White; design: DaVida Pools (bottom)

p. 195: © Lee Anne White; design: Robert Norris

p. 196: © Lee Anne White (top and bottom)

p. 197: Marylee Pangman

p. 198: Lucy Hardiman (left and right)

p. 199: © Lee Anne White; design: Lucinda Hutson (left); Lucy Hardiman (right)

p. 200: Virginia Small, courtesy Fine Gardening magazine, © The Taunton Press, Inc. (left); © Lee Anne White; design: Jeni Webber (right)

p. 201: Brandi Spade, courtesy Fine Gardening magazine, © The Taunton Press, Inc.

p. 202: © Lee Anne White (top and bottom)

p. 203: Deanne Fortnam

p. 204: © Mick Hales (left); Todd Meier, courtesy Fine Gardening magazine, © The Taunton Press, Inc.

p. 207: Steve Cominsky, courtesy Fine Gardening magazine, © The Taunton Press, Inc.

p. 208: Brandi Spade, courtesy Fine Gardening magazine, © The Taunton Press, Inc.

p. 209: Danielle Sherry, courtesy Fine

Gardening magazine, © The Taunton Press, Inc. (left); Steve Aitken, courtesy Fine Gardening magazine, © The Taunton Press, Inc. (right)

p. 210: Brandi Spade, courtesy Fine Gardening magazine, © The Taunton Press, Inc.

p. 211: © Steve Silk (left); © Lee Anne White (right)

p. 212: Holly Lepere Photography, © Grace Design Associates (top left and top right); © Lee Anne White (bottom)

p. 213: Brandi Spade, courtesy Fine Gardening magazine, © The Taunton Press, Inc.

index

INDEX OF PLANTS

Note: Page numbers in *italics* indicate plant recipe.